From Strength to Strength

From Strength to Strength

Seven Timeless Virtues for Christian Discipleship

JOSEPH T. LaBELLE

WIPF & STOCK · Eugene, Oregon

FROM STRENGTH TO STRENGTH
Seven Timeless Virtues for Christian Discipleship

Copyright © 2020 Joseph T. LaBelle. All rights reserved. Except for brief quotations in critical publications or reviews, no part of this book may be reproduced in any manner without prior written permission from the publisher. Write: Permissions, Wipf and Stock Publishers, 199 W. 8th Ave., Suite 3, Eugene, OR 97401.

Wipf & Stock
An Imprint of Wipf and Stock Publishers
199 W. 8th Ave., Suite 3
Eugene, OR 97401

www.wipfandstock.com

PAPERBACK ISBN: 978-1-7252-6144-0
HARDCOVER ISBN: 978-1-7252-6143-3
EBOOK ISBN: 978-1-7252-6145-7

Manufactured in the U.S.A.   07/01/20

All biblical quotations are from the New Revised Standard Version (NRSV).

All quranic quotations are from *The Holy Qur-Ān: English Translation of the Meaning and Commentary*. King Fahd Holy Qur-An Printing Complex, 1994.

Contents

Acknowledgments	*vii*
List of Abbreviations	*ix*
Introduction	*xi*
1. Patience for Participating in the Hidden Divine Plan	1
2. Humility and Grateful Living in the Reign of God	23
3. Christian Obedience to the Authority of Christ	46
4. Chastity Leading to Deeper Christian Love	68
5. Voluntary Poverty for Greater Availability to the Spirit	94
6. Fortitude for Steadfast Christian Discipleship	115
7. Christian Gratitude to Nurture a Thankful Life	135
Bibliography	*161*
Name Index	*167*

Acknowledgments

THE PRODUCTION OF THIS book over several years has benefitted from many discussions and conversations with colleagues and others from Oblate School of Theology and beyond. In particular, I wish to thank Linda Gibler, OP, Ronald Quillo, and Dale Schlitt, OMI, for their time spent in editing, proofreading, and offering suggestions. I also thank Renata Furst, John Markey, OP, and Ronald Rolheiser, OMI, for their advice and encouragement, and Carmen Rodriguez of the Donald E. O'Shaughnessy Library for her assistance.

I also wish to thank my Missionary Oblate brothers of our Oblate Madonna retirement community, with whom I lived for several years and who were interested in the project. Finally, thanks to the members of my present Eugene de Mazenod faculty community for their listening to my comments and musings during the long course of producing this work.

List of Abbreviations

ANF	*Ante-Nicene Fathers: The Writings of the Fathers Down to A.D. 325*. Edited by Alexander Roberts and James Donaldson. 10 vols. Peabody, MA: Hendrickson, 1994.
b.	born
Baker	*Baker Encyclopedic Dictionary of the Bible*. Edited by Walter A. Elwell et al. 4 vols. Grand Rapids: Baker, 1997.
ca.	*circa*, approximately
chap.	chapter
d.	died
EBT	*Encyclopedia of Biblical Theology: The Complete Sacramentum Verbi*. Edited by J. B. Bauer. 3 vols. New York: Crossroad, 1981.
no.	number
NPNF1	*Nicene and Post-Nicene Fathers*. First series. Edited by Philip Schaff. 14 vols. Peabody, MA: Hendrickson, 1994.
NPNF2	*Nicene and Post-Nicene Fathers: A Select Library of Nicene and Post-Nicene Fathers of the Christian Church*. Second series. Edited by Philip Schaff and Henry Wace. 14 vols. Grand Rapids: Eerdmans, 1968.
para.	paragraph
RB	*The Rule of Benedict: An Introduction to the Christian Life*, by Georg Holzherr and translated by Mark Thamert. Cistercian Studies Series 256. Collegeville: Liturgical, 2016.
Summa	*Summa Theologica of St. Thomas Aquinas*. 3 vols. New York: Benziger, 1947.

List of Abbreviations

TDNT *Theological Dictionary of the New Testament.* Edited by Gerhard Kittel and Gerhard Friedrich. Translated by Geoffrey W. Bromiley. 10 vols. Grand Rapids: Eerdmans, 1964–76.

Introduction

Happy are those whose strength is in you,
in whose heart are the highways to Zion.
As they go through the valley of Baca they make it a place of springs;
the early rain also covers it with pools.
They go from strength to strength; the God of gods will be seen in Zion.

—*Psalm 84:5–7*

"A book on *virtues*?" you may ask.

Among the myriad publications in contemporary Christian spirituality over the past fifty years, relatively little has been written on the importance of moral virtues in Christian discipleship and ministry. Virtues, in a nutshell, comprise a set of classically-recognized human qualities (or "strengths" from the Latin *virtus*). When interiorly cultivated over time, virtues become habitual ways of living and help to foster one's realization of what the ancient Greeks called the "happy life." For Christians, the truly happy life is one that follows the lived example and teaching of Jesus. Over time, an extensive list of Christian virtues developed that were apparent in Jesus' life, and have been practiced by countless Christian disciples ever since.

For many contemporary people, the concept of virtue has perhaps been consigned to the attic of Roman Catholic tradition along with other items and practices of a bygone past. Indeed, the understanding of "virtue" is a somewhat murky one, sometimes the object of incorrect understanding and abuse, and therefore to be approached with some caution. Just what is a virtue? How may virtues fit into a Christian spiritual life without becoming mired in theological discourse? What are some of the specifically Christian

Introduction

virtues that have a long tradition of practice and evolution in understanding, as opposed to more contemporary human qualities that are presented as virtues, worthwhile as they may be?

Appreciation for the seven Christian virtues in this book evolved over the long history of Christian spirituality. The Hebrew Scripture does not speak significantly of virtue before the influence of Greek thought in the later Old Testament period, likely due to the Hellenist influence on Alexandrian Jewish mysticism. The New Testament writings exhort Christians to cultivate Paul's "fruit of the Spirit" of "love, joy, peace, patience, kindness, generosity, faithfulness, gentleness, and self-control" (Gal 5:22–23). Christian appreciation for the four key or "cardinal" virtues of prudence, justice, temperance, and fortitude grew during the following centuries through the later medieval period, eventually leading to what we might recognize as the traditionally recognized list of Christian virtues found in the thirteenth-century writings of Scholastic theology and notably of Thomas Aquinas. This new systematic approach to virtues of Christian living resulted in a more abstract theological basis for understanding virtues, contrary to the longer Christian practiced (or practical) tradition that was rooted in experiences of daily life and prayer. This "newer" list grew to dominate the study of virtue in Christian theology and asceticism until the middle twentieth century, with the reawakened interest in Christian spiritual experience as the way to pursue virtue and holiness.

The sixteenth through twentieth centuries produced several written ascetical manuals that addressed the importance of select virtues and specific ways to cultivate them, through the insight of spiritual writers including Alphonsus Rodriguez (1526–1616), Francis de Sales (1567–1622), Jean-Jacques Olier (1608–1657), Adolph Tanquerey (1854–1932), and Reginald Garrigou-Legrange (1877–1964). These works had a significant impact on the practical spiritual life of countless devout Christians until the 1960s and the many changes of the Second Vatican Council. Following a period of evolution in moral theology that seemed to have given less emphasis to moral virtue development, interest in classical virtue was revived somewhat following the publishing in 1981 of *After Virtue*, the influential work by Alistair MacIntyre (1929–present).

The seven chosen Christian virtues are among those frequently mentioned in historical works and other texts reaching back to the earliest followers of Jesus. Patience (indeed a virtue as the old saying goes) allows us to live and walk in the often-frustrating mysterious ways through which God

Introduction

leads each person, calling on resources of trust in the divine vision that beholds the entirety of our life and the vastness of the universe. Humility recalls us to our commonality with all the human family, all of us as sons and daughters of the same heavenly Father, leading us to a greater respect of one another and better care of creation that we all hold in our hands. Obedience led Jesus to trust deeply in the unfailing providential love of his heavenly Father to whom Jesus was totally dedicated in reciprocal love; contemporary Christian obedience, while leading us to love God above all things, also fosters greater respect for the divine norms of nature and the universe by which all creation is held in balance and motion. Chastity, rather than being a negatively-understood restriction on sexual pleasure, recognizes and respects that human creativity and love may be expressed through many outlets, channels for the powerful and creative divine love at our center. Voluntary poverty aims to free us from the excessive desire and human recognition that we may seek through created things, so to be more sensitive to the divine movements that call us to a greater love of others. Fortitude, one of the four aforementioned cardinal virtues, is also a moral one that fosters personal courage and the willingness to endure suffering and fear for the sake of honoring or protecting something cherished, the greatest of which being for God as our greatest good. Gratitude, finally, can lead us to cultivate lives that are rooted in thankfulness to God for all of our blessings, including the invaluable gift of our faith.

Three of these—chastity, poverty, and obedience—are, in fact, practiced in a particular and focused manner by certain Roman Catholic individuals who commit themselves to follow Jesus more closely by cultivating these virtues as lifelong vows, according to their particular calling and lifestyle. For the vast majority of Christians who do not follow these "vows of religion," *From Strength to Strength* offers a historical foundation from which to adapt each of them to one's present-day Christian circumstances and obligations, so to follow more closely the way of Jesus.

This book does not pretend to be a theological study of the proposed virtues, nor is it specifically a "how-to" manual; rather, it examines the seven qualities through the lens of practical (lived) Christian spirituality along the arc of its long history. The overall methodology for each chapter has two parts. The first offers a historical and traditional appreciation for the given virtue through the mid-twentieth century, drawing from the works of a variety of past spiritual writers from the Old and New Testaments into the Patristic Era (100–500 AD), Medieval Era (500–1500),

Introduction

Modern Era (1500–1930s), and Contemporary Era (1930s to the present). Thus equipped with a sense of the traditional understandings and value placed on the proposed virtue, the second part of the chapter searches for additional insight and examples from a range of contemporary sources (Christian and non-Christian religious traditions, secular movements, the sciences, etc.). The final chapter section proposes a contemporary vision for how the time-honored Christian virtue may be appropriated in light of God's continual engagement with our world. If our human interactions with God, each other, and the surrounding creation may be viewed as three concentric and interacting circles, the reader is encouraged to develop the given virtue from the deepest realm of the *personal* (how the virtue can affect one's interior life with God through Jesus Christ), the *interrelational* (how the virtue can affect our relationships with other persons), and the *co-creative* (how exercising the virtue can lead to our more harmonious and respectful coexistence as a part of creation).

From Strength to Strength is intended primarily for all sisters and brothers in Christ, in whatever may be their particular life situation, who seek to grow more fully into Christ through cultivating these seven time-honored dispositions. Christian pastoral leaders and students who are in training for ministry should find this work to be particularly interesting and helpful. All Christians, through our common baptism, have been reborn into the life of Christ and strive to be transformed into Christ. Although perhaps in less visible but nonetheless important lives of faithfulness, each of us is called to share the new life of the risen Christ through his or her personal lived example in the midst of family, friends, workplace, and the public square.

May the Holy Spirit continue to guide and strengthen our ongoing witness to the Good News of the risen Christ and its power to transform and strengthen us, day by day, through the events and challenges of our lives.

1

Patience for Participating in the Hidden Divine Plan

PATIENCE, PATIENCE! MUCH OF Western society suffers from a lack of patience. Long considered essential for growth in all other virtues, patience has become for many people a quaint attribute, something desirable as long as it doesn't require too much effort to attain. In the end we can find ourselves too impatient to cultivate the virtue in our world that imposes increasing demands on our time, this despite the offerings of a seductive electronic "gadget culture" that tantalizes us with an endless line of supposedly time-saving devices.

For disciples of Jesus, the Christian virtue of patience enables us to bear physical and moral sufferings without sadness of spirit or dejection of heart. It is one of the most necessary virtues in the Christian life, sustaining us in the daily pursuit of Christian discipleship and fulfillment of our personal potential.

I. CHRISTIAN PATIENCE THROUGH THE CENTURIES

Patience in Scriptures

The Old Testament

The English word, from the Latin *pati* (to suffer), has several different understandings in the Scriptures. Two are especially noteworthy for us, as they appear in both the Old and New Testaments.

One interpretation of the Old Testament usage denotes a steadfast calmness of spirit despite a severe provocation to lose one's temper, typically using the phrase "slow to anger." God gives the quintessential example, as revealed to Moses:

> The LORD passed before him, and proclaimed, "The LORD, the LORD, a God merciful and gracious, slow to anger, and abounding in steadfast love and faithfulness, keeping steadfast love for the thousandth generation, forgiving iniquity and transgression and sin, yet by no means clearing the guilty, but visiting the iniquity of the parents upon the children and the children's children, to the third and the fourth generation."[1]

The belief that God willfully assigns divine punishment upon a sinner's offspring would eventually fade from Hebrew experience; the main point of this passage is that God prefers to be exceedingly patient with a sinner in hope that the person might eventually return to God.

The Wisdom author exhorts God's people to remain in true worship of God and not turn to empty idols because "you, our God, are kind and true, patient, and ruling all things in mercy. For even if we sin we are yours, knowing your power" (Wis 15:1–2). Without dismissing God's wrath against evildoers who show no willingness to repent, the author also teaches that God is patient for the sake of weak human sinners so that they may finally turn to God with all their heart:

> Like a drop of water from the sea and a grain of sand,
> so are a few years among the days of eternity.
> That is why the Lord is patient with them and pours out his mercy upon them.
> He sees and recognizes that their end is miserable;
> therefore he grants them forgiveness all the more.

---

1. Exod 34:6–8.

> The compassion of human beings for their neighbors, but the compassion of the Lord is for every living thing...
> He has compassion on those who accept his discipline and who are eager for his precepts.[2]

The author of third Isaiah comforted the Hebrew people as he recalled them from their exile to rebuild the temple and return to pious living in Jerusalem, reminding them that "the LORD waits to be gracious to you; therefore he exalts himself to show mercy to you. For the LORD is a God of justice; blessed are all those who wait for him" (Isa 30:18).

A second important Greek sense of patience describes when a person remains firm under trials, similar to the English qualities of longsuffering, steadfastness, or sometimes perseverance. God's people were exhorted to practice this attribute through patiently enduring God's mysterious and continually unfolding plan for their salvation. One who succeeds in doing so will be blessed, as Sirach observes: "Those who are patient stay calm until the right moment, and then cheerfulness comes back to them. They hold back their words until the right moment; and the lips of many tell of their good sense" (1:23–24).

In the account of righteous Job, losing all of his possessions and family left him sorely tempted to despair of his God for what he considered incomprehensible divine actions toward him. Job's perseverance, however, despite his eventual lashing out at God toward the end of the story, led to his acceptance of God's unfathomable manner of interacting with creation. It won for him an abundance of blessing, signified by receiving back twice what he had lost.

The New Testament

The New Testament authors more commonly utilized this sense of enduring patience or longsuffering, fully exemplified in the life and passion of Jesus. Just as Christ endured in maintaining to the end his fidelity to his Father, so his disciples are exhorted to endure the difficulties of following their master and thereby find his new life offered through the Paschal mystery.

Longsuffering (enduring patience) became the principal understanding of patience in the early Christian centuries. Several significant living conditions shaped the Christian appreciation for longsuffering: the

---

2. Sir 18:10–14.

oftentimes difficult coexistence between Jewish Christians and the growing number of Greek-speaking gentile converts; the struggle for unity within the churches with the apparent delay of Christ's return and subsequent restlessness in the churches; and the continual threat of persecution and periodic eruptions of martyrdom from the latter first through early fourth centuries. The apostle Paul encountered each of these obstacles during his Christian life, both personally and among the Christian communities with whom he corresponded. His letter to the newly-converted of the Thessalonica community encouraged them to hold fast for the life of the community:

> Be at peace among yourselves. And we urge you, beloved, to admonish the idlers, encourage the fainthearted, help the weak, be patient with all of them. See that none of you repays evil for evil, but always seek to do good to one another and to all.[3]

He exhorted the Colossians to a sincere following of Christ through imitating Jesus while guided by love for one another:

> As God's chosen ones, holy and beloved, clothe yourselves with compassion, kindness, humility, meekness, and patience. Bear with one another and, if anyone has a complaint against another, forgive each other; just as the Lord has forgiven you, so you also must forgive. Above all, clothe yourselves with love, which binds everything together in perfect harmony.[4]

Scriptural documents of the later first century frequently exhorted their readers toward enduring patience. The first two chapters of Revelation extended encouragement to "the seven churches of Asia," each center with its difficulties but each exhorted to hold fast to the faith in the presence of false prophets, persecution, and the threat of being led astray by the surrounding paganism. The author asserted that God's kingdom would finally be realized despite the purifying evil with which their oppressors may assail them, "for God has put it into their hearts to carry out his purpose by agreeing to give their kingdom to the beast, until the words of God will be fulfilled" (Rev 17:17).

The late-first-century letter to the Hebrews recalls the life and death of Jesus as the truly unique high priest who offered himself as a sacrifice to atone for our sins, the mediator of the New Covenant between God and God's people (Heb 9:15) and deserving of our confidence (10:21–22).

---

3. 1 Thess 5:13b–15.
4. Col 3:12–14.

Patience for Participating in the Hidden Divine Plan

The author exhorts the readers to imitate the Savior's attitude of enduring hardship while remaining confident of the Father's love, even to death if one be so called, recalling the steadfast lives of earlier faith-filled heroes such as Noah, Moses, and Abraham, and perfectly revealed in that of Jesus (11:1–40). The suffering of the Son of God gives hope to all who are challenged to be steadfast in their faith:

> Let us run with perseverance the race that is set before us, looking to Jesus the pioneer and perfecter of our faith, who for the sake of the joy that was set before him endured the cross, disregarding its shame, and has taken his seat at the right hand of the throne of God . . . Consider him who endured such hostility against himself from sinners, so that you may not grow weary or lose heart.[5]

This theme of imitating Jesus is also found in 2 Timothy 2:11–13 and 3:10.

Other pastoral letters reveal that the Christian community had grown to appreciate other positive reasons for practicing Jesus' enduring patience. Such endurance will bring one to a greater maturity in faith (Jas 1:2; 1 Pet 4:12; 2 Pet 1:3–7). The letter of Jude, addressed to a Christian community beset by verbal scoffers and others who offered conflicting doctrines, exhorts its members to hold fast to their faith and virtuous behavior while awaiting God's justice, thereby offering testimony to the power of faith in divine deliverance:

> But you, beloved, build yourselves up on your most holy faith; pray in the Holy Spirit; keep yourselves in the love of God; look forward to the mercy of our Lord Jesus Christ that leads to eternal life. And have mercy on some who are wavering; save others by snatching them out of the fire; and have mercy on still others with fear, hating even the tunic defiled by their bodies.[6]

The New Testament also recognizes the Hebrew regard for patience as a divine attribute, though less frequently used. In Matthew 18:26, the slave who was forgiven his debt by his slow-to-anger master was chastised for being impatient with another who owed him a much smaller amount. Just as God our master has shown great tolerance for our debts, so we should practice this same patience toward others.

---

5. Heb 12:2–3.
6. Jude 1:20–23.

The second letter of Peter, written perhaps a hundred years after the life of Christ, was concerned with bolstering and reanimating a Christian community to renewed watchfulness for the coming day of the Lord. The author pointedly reminds the audience that God's great patience toward them in not having yet returned was for the sake of their redemption; it should not, however, be taken for granted:

> But do not ignore this one fact, beloved, that with the Lord one day is like a thousand years, and a thousand years are like one day. The Lord is not slow about his promise, as some think of slowness, but is patient with you, not wanting any to perish, but all to come to repentance. But the day of the Lord will come like a thief, and the heavens will pass away with a loud noise, and the elements will be dissolved with fire, and the earth and everything that is done on it will be disclosed.[7]

Patience in the Patristic Era

The Church Fathers

The early patristic writings offer many appeals to cultivate patient endurance. The first letter to the Corinthians by Clement, bishop of Rome (d. ca. 101 AD), exhorted the fractious church at Corinth to return to their earlier life of communal peace and harmony. The impatience of some members, having grown restless and skeptical of Christ's imminent return, had brought discord and division. The bishop asserted that such complacency in past ages had provoked the evils of envy that had proved fatal to a long line of heroes among the people of God; first to Abel, later to Saul; and centuries later it would prove likewise to Jesus, Peter, and Paul among many others. Their lives each offered an example of patient endurance for the fulfillment of God's plan.[8] This plan included their growth in the love of Christ, requiring humility and obedience, but would result in communal peace and fraternal love among its members. Waiting in peace for the return of Christ is a call to enduring patience not unlike the slow progress of years and seasons:

---

7. 2 Pet 3:8–10.
8. 1 Clem. 3–6.

> May the Scripture text never apply to us that says: Wretched are the double-minded, who doubt in their heart and say: "We have heard these things even in the days of our Fathers; but, mark you, we have grown old and nothing of all this has happened to us!" You fools! Compare yourselves to a tree. Take a vine: first it sheds its foliage; then it puts forth a bud; then a leaf; then a flower; and after that, a green, sour grape; finally, there is a bunch of fresh, ripe grapes." You see, it takes but a short time to bring the fruit of the plant to maturity. In truth, quickly and suddenly will His will be accomplished, as also the Scripture testifies when it says: Quickly will he come and will not tarry; and suddenly will the Lord come to His temple—the Holy One, for whom you are looking.[9]

Patience rooted in the divine was a theme among many of the patristic authors and considered an essential virtue for anyone who aspired to follow the precepts of the Lord. Tertullian (ca. 160–ca. 225), a lay Christian apologist and theologian who wrote in characteristically sharp and often polemic verse, regarded God's forbearance as the representative example of divine patience. For Tertullian, God's patience was operative in all areas of creation; in universal forbearance with human folly and dissipation over worthless material things, over the wicked and the just, and with the slow and relentless progression of the seasons. These observations served as evidence that true patience had a divine source.[10]

Patience finds its perfection in the divinity, and Jesus offered the divine example in a way that could be humanly perceived as testimony to God's glory. This was most apparent in his passion and death:

> He is spitted on, scourged, derided, clad foully, more foully crowned. Wondrous is the faith of equanimity! He who had set before Him the concealing of Himself in man's shape, imitated nought of man's impatience! Hence, even more than from any other trait, ought you, Pharisees, to have recognised the Lord. Patience of this kind none of men would achieve.[11]

The quality of impatience, detrimental to following the way of discipleship and corrosive to Christian life, conversely finds its root in the evil one, the source of all evil, whose impatience stemmed from God having

---

9. 1 Clem. 23, 24.
10. Tertullian, *Pat.* 2.
11. Tertullian, *Pat.* 3.

gifted humanity with the divine image.[12] Indeed, impatience for Tertullian was the foundational or cardinal vice of the devil and conduit of all evil. The root source of the fall of Adam and Eve, impatience remains forever within humanity and has the effect of thwarting human attainment of peace and full happiness.[13]

Patience is so important to Tertullian because one's gradually maturing faith in God, tried in the crucible of daily life, depends upon its cultivation. Our willingness to trust in God's care for us is tested in cases of personal injustice done to us, whether in moments of grief over the loss of a loved one or in times of persecution or mistreatment because of our faith. Patience in such moments is also a remedy against committing further evil. Ultimately, we are exhorted to have faith in the hands of the One who holds all of creation and patiently awaits its fulfillment while accompanying us in our adversity. Our exercise of patience points toward its divine source, "for where God is, there too is his foster-child, namely Patience. When God's spirit descends, then Patience accompanies Him indivisibly."[14]

Another Carthaginian by way of his episcopacy, Cyprian (200–258) is often considered a spiritual master of patience. The occasional third-century persecution of Christians was beginning to tear apart some of the African church communities. The struggle during the reign of Decian had also left a deep wound in the African church between those who had kept the Christian faith and individuals (including bishops and deacons) who had submitted to anti-Christian demands, including the surrender of liturgical books and sacred vessels. Awaiting the return of Christ and final divine judgement on the Romans had become difficult. It was within this context that Cyprian wrote *On the Advantage of Patience*.

Cyprian was a reader of Tertullian's works and there is a striking similarity between the two texts. Missing, however, is Tertullian's linguistic directness found in his theological writing. An outstanding theologian as well as a gifted preacher, Cyprian used a more inviting and image-filled style to illustrate that the fullness of patience is found in the divinity.

> But what and how great is the patience in God, that, most patiently enduring the profane temples and the images of earth, and the sacrilegious rites instituted by men, in contempt of His majesty and

---

12. Tertullian, *Pat.* 5.

13. See Steenberg, "Impatience and Humanity's Sinful State in Tertullian," 117–18 (esp. n35).

14. Tertullian, *Pat.* 15.

> honour, He makes the day to begin and the light of the sun to arise alike upon the good and the evil; and while He waters the earth with showers, no one is excluded from His benefits, but upon the righteous equally with the unrighteous He bestows His undiscriminating rains . . . and while God is provoked with frequent, yea, with continual offenses, He softens His indignation, and in patience waits for the day of retribution, once for all determined; and although He has revenge in His power, He prefers to keep patience for a long while, bearing, that is to say, mercifully, and putting off, so that, if it might be possible, the long protracted mischief may at some time be changed, and man, involved in the contagion of errors and crimes, may even though late be converted to God . . .[15]

For Cyprian, Jesus was also the exemplar of divine patience throughout his life, ultimately revealed in his passion. His unjust suffering and death were necessary "even to the end, all things are borne perseveringly and constantly, in order that in Christ a full and perfect patience may be consummated."[16]

While Tertullian recognized that patience is a necessary antecedent to faith, Cyprian regarded the virtue as necessary both to faith as well as future hope:

> We must endure and persevere, beloved brethren, in order that, being admitted to the hope of truth and liberty, we may attain to the truth and liberty itself; for that very fact that we are Christians is the substance of faith and hope. But that hope and faith may attain to their result, there is need of patience. For we are not following after present glory, but future, according to what Paul the apostle also warns us, and says, We are saved by hope; but hope that is seen is not hope: for what a man sees, why does he hope for? But if we hope for that which we see not, then do we by patience wait for it. Therefore, waiting and patience are needful, that we may fulfil that which we have begun to be, and may receive that which we believe and hope for, according to God's own showing.[17]

All of this is directed toward the growth of charity within and among the body of believers, "the bond of brotherhood, the foundation of peace, the holdfast and security of unity."[18] Patience is essential for this charity to endure and grow.

---

15. Cyprian, *Pat.* 4.
16. Cyprian, *Pat.* 7.
17. Cyprian, *Pat.* 13.
18. Cyprian, *Pat.* 15.

From Strength to Strength

Patient endurance bore a particular urgency during its first three centuries of intermittent Christian persecution. Christian discipleship in this early stage called for a special determination in adopting a way of life often considered foreign to non-Christians and even subversive of the Roman imperial culture. Following the life example of Jesus through exile, suffering, and gruesome martyrdom became a familiar and privileged way for disciples to imitate their master in accepting his passion and death. Patience would nourish a courageous perseverance in following the Christian way, as noted by the third-century bishop and soon-to-be martyr Polycarp (d. ca. 135):

> Let us, therefore, become imitators of the patience of Christ and if it should happen that we have to suffer on account of his name, then let us glorify him for it. This is the model which he has established for us by his own example and we must put our faith in it.[19]

Patient endurance, exercised in daily faithfulness, became recognized as the essential quality of accepting the cross and following Christ more deeply, regardless of whether one would be required to suffer physically for the faith. The total self-gift of Christian martyrdom subsequently emerged as a particular *type* or paradigm of Christian holiness by which all disciples of Jesus could spiritually participate in his mortifying passion and death through accepting the demands of their particular life circumstances.

Several notable Christian apologists addressed the difficulty that Christianity posed to the surrounding culture by way of rhetoric and reason. One of these, the Latin writer Lactantius (d. ca. 325), brought together Christian wisdom and insights from the Roman classical figures such as Cicero just before the end of the early persecutions. After arguing that pagan philosophy could not grasp the sublime wisdom of the Christian way, he offered a catechesis for Christian readers in the face of suffering and martyrdom. Lactantius proposed that personal virtues are developed only in the face of adversity; growth in patience, for him the greatest of virtues, required the imposition of the most severe and unbearable injustices. The absence of any adversity whatsoever would lead only to the absence of patience; someone who is materially rich and lacking in nothing and consequently free from any adversity was least able to develop this most essential of virtues.[20]

---

19. Polycarp, *Philippians* 9–10. Casey, "Virtue of Patience," 7.
20. Lactantius, *Inst.* 5.23.

Patience for Participating in the Hidden Divine Plan

Noting that the Christian is called to live justly with all people, Lactantius made an interesting observation. A good person, choosing to express revenge toward another, acts in the manner of a dog or other animal that merely reacts to an attack by attacking in return; such persons forfeit their goodness. One who is *truly* good is also wise and has grasped in adversity the wisdom of following in the way of Christ. Such a person will always choose patience over revenge of any kind.[21] The thought of Lactantius, together with that of several other patristic church fathers, contributed to the developing Christian tradition of nonviolence.

Early Christian Monasticism

Endurance in periods of persecution was a primary concern for early Christian churches through the early fourth century and the normalization of the Christian faith throughout the Constantinian Empire. In the wake of the persecutions there arose a sort of Christian malaise; gone were the risks of becoming a Christian as the religion became increasingly interwoven with the surrounding cultures, and fewer were the opportunities to follow Jesus so radically as in persecution and martyrdom. The resulting spiritual dissipation helped to nurture the early Christian practice of monasticism in which, initially, adherents would venture into the wilderness for an unencumbered life to seek God and overcome whatever personal weaknesses or sinfulness that impeded this. Along with the movements of dedicated Christian virginity, such embodiments of Christian asceticism became appreciated as means to follow a daily course of voluntary martyrdom and unite oneself to Christ in his self-denying passion and death into new life through a program of virtue and contemplation. This spiritual arena of self-denial became the new primary locus for the pursuit of personal holiness that would further the Christian understanding of patience.

Monastic life of solitude in the wilderness offered a continuous lifelong exercise of patience in the day-to-day, month-by-month, year-after-year pursuit of self-mastery over temptation in the pursuit of spiritual union with God. John Cassian (d. ca. 435), a key figure of early western monasticism, considered patience as essential for a monk's perseverance in solitude. He exhorted the practice of humility, obedience, meekness, and longsuffering as means to preserve a monk's peace and solitude that stood

---

21. Lactantius, *Inst.* 6.18.

to be laid waste by any unrecognized anger in the soul.²² All of this offered the cross upon which the monk would be daily crucified as a living martyr.²³ Benedict of Nursia (480–503) likewise regarded patience as essential for following his rule for communal monastic life, whether as abbot or novice, and a prospective monk should be especially tested in the latter to determine fitness for the life.²⁴ The sixth-century Gregory the Great (540–604), called to be pope while a Benedictine monk and perhaps Western monasticism's greatest proponent of his era, echoed the earliest Christian regard for patience as the key to growth in charity and all goodness.²⁵

Patience in Later Medieval Developments

Tenth-century Christian spirituality experienced a notable emphasis on the humanity of Christ, chiefly within communities of clerical canons but also within Cistercian monastic renewal, notably through Bernard of Clairvaux (1090–1153). Renewed emphasis on the humanity of Christ would also result in the emergence of several new forms of organized religious life for both consecrated men and women, such as the Franciscans, as well as a number of less-institutionally-bound groups of lay Christians. Their great desire to offer a credible Christ-centered testimony of lifestyle to accompany their preaching ministry focused upon the human and ministerial life of Jesus and that of the early apostles, with a concern to unite oneself with Jesus through cultivating his human virtues. The phenomenon was also a reaction to the growing influence of scholastic theology that many felt had become detached from practical Christian spirituality.

Later medieval Christian spirituality produced several works underscoring the importance of patience. One notable source of practical Christian spirituality, the *Devotio moderna* of the so-called "Low Countries" (present-day Netherlands, Luxembourg, and Belgium), emphasized the imitation of Jesus through daily prayer devotions and scriptural reflection. Unconcerned to achieve mystical movements or lofty experiences, its adherents were drawn to experience the virtues of Christ in key moments of his life and notably his passion, so to find greater life in Christ. A disciple wishing to do this cannot avoid accepting the cross of Jesus at particular

---

22. Casey, "Virtue of Patience," 10.
23. Casey, "Virtue of Patience," 10.
24. RB 58.
25. Gregory the Great, *Pastoral Care* 3.9.

moments of his or her life. Indeed, patiently embracing the cross in a spirit of union with Jesus crucified is salutary, as noted by Geert Groot, an influential figure in the movement:

> Alas, many of us freely take up a cross which we have made for ourselves, such as a hair-shirt or private prayers or extraordinary fasts, but that which God makes for us, also truly ours to be borne and embraced, we not only fail to take up voluntarily but cast from us in horror. For truly whatever pain we suffer at the hands of some greater, equal, or lesser power, and with whatever intention, just or unjust, on the part of the doers, they also come upon us justly and piously from the hand of God . . . It is therefore all the more meritorious and salvation-bringing, indeed all the more necessary, that we bear such crosses without resistance or murmuring and hold for naught by comparison all those things others subject us to, however laudable in their own time.[26]

The well-known work from this period, *The Imitation of Christ*, also addresses the issue of patiently bearing whatever difficulty may arise in a spirit of identification with the cross of Christ:

> Set out, then, as a good and faithful servant of Christ, to bear . . . the cross of your Lord, that cross to which he was nailed for love of you. Be prepared to endure much thwarting and many a difficulty in this life of sadness; because that's how things are going to be for you, wherever you are, that's how you're sure to find things, wherever you look for shelter from them. That's the way it's got to be; there's no cure, no getting round the fact of trouble and sorrow; you just have to put up with them. If you long to be the Lord's friend, to share what is his, you must drink his cup and like it . . . for what we suffer in this present life is nothing when we compare it with the glory to be won in the life to come.[27]

Patience in the Modern Era

Church Reform and the Reaction against Stoic Patience

Early Christian regard for patience was inevitably shaped by the cultural, religious, and philosophical influences of its day. One of these was Stoicism,

26. From a letter on patience and the imitation of Christ. Van Engen, *Devotio Moderna*, 88.
27. à Kempis, *Imitation* 2.12.

affecting patristic thought and influencing several branches of Christian spirituality through the twentieth century. Many of the citations in this chapter bear at least a faint imprint of the Greek philosophical school that considered patience as a necessary virtue leading one to union with the divine through the perfection of *apathea* ("passionlessness") and a quiet, unemotional shouldering of life's trials and inconveniences. To be sure, fatalistic Stoic patience contrasted with the patristic Christian understanding that, as with every virtue, found its root in the divine and was lived in Christian hope. The distinction became blurred at certain historical moments, however, until the Christian Reformation challenged the position through the thought of John Calvin (1509–64).[28]

Reformed Christianity generally followed Calvin's lead in avoiding a Stoic approach to the virtue, while Catholic thought witnessed a renewed Stoic influence by the later seventeenth century that would continue into the twentieth. Catholic reform spirituality also further deepened its spiritual attraction to the passion and cross of Jesus in a Christianized form of *dolorism* (the acceptance of personal pain and suffering that, when patiently accepted, can lead to a spiritual good).[29]

Modern-Era Mystics

The Carmelite mystic Teresa of Avila (1515–82) recounted in her autobiography how she struggled to follow a life of prayer and the prompting of the Holy Spirit while living in a convent in need of religious reform. Convincing others of this noble pursuit became her great focus for some time; it led, after much hardship, to Teresa's foundation of the first reformed Carmelite convents in Spain that subsequently influenced all of western Europe.

Before this, however, Teresa had to convince her superiors and confessors of the need for her holy pursuit. She was left at times wondering if some of her mystical experiences and spiritual movements were indeed from God or, as others suggested, were diabolical delusions. Teresa slowly discovered through experience that the path of patient and trusting obedience to God in spite of her misgivings was an important element of discernment. If the prompting were indeed from God, for example, she believed

---

28. Spanneut, "Le Stoïcisme," 114.
29. Spanneut, "Le Stoïcisme," 114–21.

that reluctant superiors would ultimately be moved to give their approval to her efforts.[30]

The venerated Francis de Sales (1567–1622), known as a saintly bishop of Geneva in his ministry as a kind pastor and spiritual director/confessor, had great sensitivity to the particular circumstances of each person who approached him. He recognized that one practicing patience was well-served in three ways: the person in so doing would be giving glory to God, its practice could also serve as a form of prayer, and exercising the virtue would be partaking in Jesus' passion and death:

> We must often recall that our Lord has saved us by his suffering and endurance and that we must work out our salvation by sufferings and afflictions, enduring with all possible meekness the injuries, denials, and discomforts we meet.[31]

Those exercising patience have the occasion, in their own way, to imitate the patience of Jesus and honor the sufferings of the early Christian martyrs.

> Look often with your inward eye on Christ Jesus, crucified, naked, blasphemed, slandered, forsaken, and overwhelmed by every kind of weariness, sorrow, and labor. Remember that your sufferings are not comparable to his either in quality or quantity and that you can never suffer for his sake anything equal to what he has suffered for you. Think of the torments the martyrs endured and those so many people now endure that are incomparably more grievous than yours. Then say: "Alas! Are not my hardships consolations and my thorns roses in comparison with those who without help, assistance, or relief live a continual death under the burden of afflictions infinitely greater than mine?"[32]

Later Modern-Era French and English Developments

The eighteenth and nineteenth centuries produced a number of written tracts concerning patience. Some were of a more pious nature; other works, such as the French Jean-Jacques Olier (1608–57), wrote more demandingly of the need to develop patience in his short book on select virtues and personal qualities. Olier's *Introduction to the Christian Life and Virtues*

---

30. Teresa of Avila, *Life*, chapters 32–36 and 40.
31. de Sales, *Introduction* 3.3.
32. de Sales, *Introduction* 3.3.

presents the life example of Jesus as the exemplary model for all virtue, and Olier's work offers suggestions for advancing in each. The work is heavily influenced by an Augustinian sense of duty and the need to exercise this virtue in response to God's magnificent and mysterious divinity that soars over our lowly humanity.

One nineteenth-century figure of special note was W. B. Ullathorne, who published a collection of sermons on patience. It systematically considers this virtue in relationship to that of humility. Both were dependent upon one's exercise of charity that comes to us as an expression of God's love and impels us to live and grow in every virtue. Patience gives us the fortitude to continue this journey in our life wrought with inconstancy:

> This vigorous virtue of patience is the spiritual remedy which God has provided against the weakness, perturbation, and inconstancy of our nature, exposed as it is to irritations, fears, temptations, cupidities, vanities, pride, and sadness. Every creature, by reason of its origin from nothingness, when left to itself, is exposed to division, dissolution, and failure; unless it receive a divine support, and a bracing strength of patience to hold it together, that it may endure and persevere.[33]

To summarize the historical view of patience into the twentieth century, we find that the early Christian centuries witnessed the greatest development among the church fathers who offered a richly diverse range of appreciation for the virtue. Some, such as Tertullian and Cyprian, articulated their appreciation for it as rooted in the divine and thus of particular value, made humanly known in the life and death of Jesus. It was, therefore, worthy of imitation by his disciples amidst the tensions existing between Christian cultural groups and between Christians and the wider pagan world. The practice of patience was also considered essential to growth in Christian maturity and perseverance that testified to its divine source. Patience as endurance grew to be very important in the early centuries of monasticism, becoming more valued as a practice of asceticism.

The medieval and modern eras, while offering a more narrow range of appreciation, further emphasized the practice of patience in light of following the example of Jesus' human life through emphasizing the example of his passion and death. Patience in suffering could also serve as a form of prayer.

---

33. Ullathorne, *Christian Patience*, 7.

II. TOWARDS A CONTEMPORARY APPRECIATION OF CHRISTIAN PATIENCE

Considerations of Patience outside and within Christian Practice

The virtue of patience receives little attention in the present day beyond the occasional journal article in psychology or human development. Even the Christian world, apart from infrequent devotional appeals, offers it only limited attention when compared to its first two millennia. We find, ironically, that the apparently underrated quality of patience does, in fact, find a clear place within a variety of contemporary movements and worldviews, albeit at times hidden in the guise of other concepts.

Patience traditionally has been valued within several world religions, and at least some of the reasons offered to pursue it can resonate with Christian ones. The Hindu practice of *yoga* regards patience as a virtue that allows one, when faced with the innumerable tests upon daily patience, to accept these in an attitude of ultimately looking beyond them toward greater spiritual growth. This quality of looking ahead to further advancement in the face of hardship finds a parallel in the Christian virtue of hope that also invites us to envision a fuller human life lying beyond the difficulties of a present situation. This form of patience is hardly a passive resignation but rather a potentially beneficial choice on the way to inner peace and union with the universal divine will. Nor is patience to be practiced indiscriminately toward all personal hardship but rather limited to those areas that will serve to promote one's inner transformation; it might otherwise be an escape from personal weaknesses or a denial of social disorders such as involuntary poverty or other expressions of injustice.[34]

The Buddhist view of patience is oriented to the pursuit of living in the present moment; lacking patience is an inability to accept the present life circumstance and can be strengthened through personal meditation. The Buddhist understanding of patience is significantly different from the Christian one, however. While the Christian sense of patience signifies the endurance of a difficult imposition upon an individual, Buddhist patience seeks to avoid returning harm toward oneself or another through the control of emotion.[35] One can nonetheless appreciate its similarity with the

---

34. Arundel, "Patience—A Spiritual Virtue," para. 8.
35. Rabgye, "Virtue of Patience," paras. 3–4.

early Christian maxim to practice patience rather than retaliate or otherwise cause evil.

No one, Christian or otherwise, can claim the ability to live without the need for patience in life. The unemployed who search for weeks, months, and years for meaningful employment; the recent college graduate standing at the bottom of the corporate career ladder; young parents learning to cope with the utter dependence of a first child; chronically ill persons who are left without reason for their illness and suffering and must shoulder its burden day after day; each of these remind us of the great place and need for patience. Such moments may also cause us to wonder whether we would be able to muster this inner resource. Virtually every person will find innumerable moments of need for patience at some time or other, if only in times of being helplessly ensnared in traffic jams.

The remainder of this chapter presents a contemporary Christian appreciation of patience that is rooted in Christian tradition while serving the ongoing creative work of God.

Pierre Teilhard de Chardin (1881–1955)

One integrating perspective comes by way of this Jesuit priest, mystic, theologian, and scientist. Teilhard de Chardin's system of process theology initially found a mixed and wary reception from Roman Catholic theological authorities but has found wider acceptance in the decades following Vatican II. Teilhard wrote neither of patience nor indeed of any virtue. A closer look at his thought, however, reveals a context for the practice of patience that can lead to a deeper relationship with God in Christ.

Teilhard's cosmological view was of a creation in constant evolution, always progressing from lower to higher degrees of individual development, communal integration, and divine communion, towards an ultimate point of convergent union with God. This movement has been humanly expressed through the life of Jesus Christ. After fully immersing himself into physical creation to experience the deepest possible measure of human life, Christ emerged once again from the limitations of visible temporal creation, through his passion and death, to the fullness of being and existence in union with God. This journey of Christ, in which he entered fully into creation with all its joys and deepest suffering, was only the first part of his odyssey. His experience of the passion and cross required his deepest relinquishment of self through which he realized the new life of the resurrection, bringing humankind and all of creation to the beginning of a renewed wholeness with God. This journey of Christ has offered forever afterward the paradigm for one of Teilhard's key assertions—that all of humanity, indeed all of creation including humanity, is undergoing a journey of progress from lower to higher degrees of integration. All of creation is continually evolving from lesser to greater levels of development, from its first moment of inception, its "Alpha point," until it finally converges into a still-distant "Omega point" where the reign of God will be handed over to the Father, and creation will ultimately be made subject to Christ.[36]

This endless and restless activity in creation includes *all* of creation, and humanity plays its part through its individual members. Every personal decision will have some perhaps immeasurable though definite impact upon our personal development and consequently upon our relationship with others and the surrounding world. Like it or not, we participate in the ongoing swirl of creation's progress as we hurtle toward that distant point of total integration. Our willed choice to exercise patience in a given situation is a choice to actuate something of the divine patience that has been operative from the beginning of time. It is likewise a choice to make God's love present to another, to open a door for God's love into the world around us.

At the center of Teilhard's Christ-centered spirituality stands the cross. Rather than emphasizing the crucifixion as paying the price of humanity's collective debt of sin, Teilhard asserted that the Paschal Mystery of Christ's crucifixion and resurrection to new life has resulted in an extended horizon encircling our relationship with God, with one another, and our relationship to the rest of creation. Jesus' human experience within our temporal creation has raised humanity to a new level of progress in the process of creation's evolution. His greatest expression of the capacity for human love, his passion and death, reveals our potential to fullest human integration and freedom to respond to God's love for us, love that brings us both to fullest individuality as individuals and greatest capacity for communion within the entire human community. The cross of Christ thus symbolizes the continual human movement toward ever-greater degrees of personal individuation and spiritual freedom, while slowly progressing toward our final Omega point of fullest communion of creation with God in Christ.

---

36. See 1 Cor 15:24–27. For more information on Teilhard de Chardin's thought, read Egan, *Christian Mysticism*, 260–77; Faricy, "Teilhard de Chardin's Spirituality of the Cross," 1–15; Teilhard de Chardin, *Divine Milieu*.

Recalling the sacrificial and patient love of Christ for us will help us to see the cultivation of patience as a way to participate in this ongoing journey.

Christian Patience in Relationships with God, with Others, and as Part of Creation

With God

Patience is a gift (sometimes called a "fruit") of the Holy Spirit. By our baptism, Christians are introduced through Christ into the trinitarian community of Father, Son, and Holy Spirit. We engage or "participate" in varying degree with the continual relationship of complete unselfish love between Father and Son, giving us "life in the Holy Spirit" and opening us to the Spirit's gifts. These gifts fortify us to deepen our relationship with the person of risen Christ and help us to grow toward fullness of human existence and discipleship as daughters and sons of God. We are not to live this privileged life in isolated self-fulfilment, however; we seek to become Christ so that Christ's love for others, through our love, may continue in the world for all generations. Our relationship with Christ calls us to share in Christ's continual worship of his heavenly Father through our patient self-giving in the ordinary events of our lives. The Roman Catholic papal encyclical *Lumen Gentium* from the Second Vatican Council notes that all baptized Christians are called to participate in the self-sacrifice of Christ:

> For besides intimately linking them to His life and His mission, [*Christ*] also gives them a sharing in His priestly function of offering spiritual worship for the glory of God and the salvation of men. For this reason the laity, dedicated to Christ and anointed by the Holy Spirit, are marvelously called and wonderfully prepared so that ever more abundant fruits of the Spirit may be produced in them. For all their works, prayers and apostolic endeavors, their ordinary married and family life, their daily occupations, their physical and mental relaxation, if carried out in the Spirit, and even the hardships of life, if patiently borne—all these become "spiritual sacrifices acceptable to God through Jesus Christ."[37]

---

37. Paul VI, *Lumen Gentium*, no. 34.

Patience for Participating in the Hidden Divine Plan

With Others

The final years in the life of Pope John Paul II (1920–2005) offered an inspiring model of involuntary patient suffering. Earlier in his papacy, his apostolic letter to the Catholic faithful on the Christian meaning of suffering (*Salvifici Doloris*) highlighted several aspects of suffering within the human experience that, by extension, also offer insight into the patient endurance of human hardship.

Suffering, the pope noted, is an inescapable reality of the human condition, brought to human consciousness most vividly in times of war and other disasters. Jesus Christ entered our suffering-prone world intent upon living most fully our human condition as a way for the Father's love to fully permeate all of humanity; such was God's way of redemption offered to us. Jesus' patient acceptance of his passion and crucifixion formed his fullest expression of God's loving, providential plan for us. This redemptive expression of deepest love has been achieved once and for all but remains capable of joining to itself all other human activities, suffering, or deprivations, when undertaken with an attitude of loving acceptance of God's mysterious plan for an individual. In this way, one's patient endurance of whatever suffering or other difficulty, when accepted as a love-centered act for the good of another, becomes a way of uniting one's love for another to the unselfish love of Jesus. One who offers this in faith, as Jesus did, extends his presence into today for others to see, witnessing to the way of Christ who completed his mission of love through suffering.

Our opportunities for love-centered acts are innumerable and of varying intensity, and offer moments to offer a portion of ourselves or our time as a sacrifice of love to God. Apart from the heroic suffering and patience required of the chronically ill and disabled, married individuals and parents encounter their own difficult moments. Accepting the daily minor irritations of a spouse, teaching a child to tie a shoe for the hundredth time, allowing a child or adolescent to make a mistake (hopefully minor!) in the hope that he or she will learn from the experience . . . the list goes on. Those who live a ministerial vocation likewise have no shortage of opportunities calling for self-sacrificing patience. The need for patience is part of our human condition, and its acceptance as a loving act will lead us to an exercise of transcendent good through an offering of prayer and solidarity with Christ in his ongoing redemptive and patient love of all humanity. This solidarity also unites us with all those in the world who must endure the fatigue and inconvenience of patience in their own circumstances.

From Strength to Strength

As Part of Creation

The rest of creation surrounding us is no stranger to requiring enormous amounts of time and patience as it slowly progresses from one developmental stage to another. The vast number of Earth-years required for the individual planets to achieve their forms and orbits around the sun; the barely perceptible movement of the earth's continental plates as they continually push one another toward some distant moment of stability; the seasonal pace by which agricultural produce develops from seed to maturity; each of these reveals that patience is innate to creation and, hence, to us as temporal created beings. Creation—including humanity, world, and universe—is evolving from lesser to greater unification and harmony. As with all of creation but as privileged creatures due to the image of God that we each carry as human beings, we participate by our actions in this ongoing spiral dance even though unaware of it. The patience that we exercise for the good of others serves to extend the love of Christ to them, thereby aiding in their ongoing development that is tied inescapably to the ceaseless change of all creation as it progresses upward toward the return of Christ at the last day.

A more deliberate, purposeful, and prayerful resignation to exercise patience, regardless of whether or not we find ourselves with a choice in the matter, allows us to follow the example of Jesus who trusted in his heavenly father's love in moments of patient endurance. In so doing, contemporary disciples open themselves to the unknowable divine plan while trusting in God's love, especially in their most trying and even painful moments.

2

Humility and Grateful Living in the Reign of God

THE CHRISTIAN UNDERSTANDING OF humility, in a nutshell, is living with the recognition that God is our creator and that we depend entirely on God for everything in our lives. It is an essential attitude for those seeking to follow Jesus' life example. Once considered by spiritual masters to be the primary moral virtue before others, the virtue of humility in recent decades has tended to be more a subject of discussion within the realm of psychology than Christian spiritual life. Within the Roman Catholic experience, memories of pre-Vatican II observances of humility in seminary and religious spiritual formation programs, with their occasionally misguided practices of so-called "humiliations," have subsequently given the virtue an unwelcome scent that has yet to dissipate.

Authentic humility, as we understand it today, is an elusive quality—not only because of the usual difficulty in acquiring and refining of any virtue, but also because one cannot know when one *has* done so. In some ways it is like trying to capture darkness in a small box; the moment that we begin to look for it by opening the box, light enters and the darkness disappears. Humility firmly acquired will have an unconscious quality to it, as the person who has it will not be aware that it is present.

From Strength to Strength

I. CHRISTIAN HUMILITY THROUGH THE CENTURIES

The word humility is translated from the Latin *humilitas* and shares the same root as the Latin word *humus*, meaning soil or earth. The early moral quality of *humilitas* takes its understanding from the ancient Greek senses of the word that conveyed such ideas as a personal state of lowliness, weakness, or insignificance. Indeed, the Latin word referred to one's subservient attitude toward others, conveyed by one's bowing or kneeling, or lowering one's gaze to the ground. In practice, it commonly referred to one's standing in relationship to another, be it a military defeat, an occupying ruler, or perhaps to a deity. The idea of practicing humility was contemptible in light of the ancient Greek understanding that men were intended to be free and autonomous beings. With such cultural understandings, the humility of Jesus would be a stumbling-block among Greek-speaking Christians during its first centuries.

Humility in Scriptures

The Old Testament

Within the Hebrew religious world, the idea of humility and particularly one's action of humiliating another person or oneself had a much richer spiritual character, thanks in part to their many communal experiences of defeat, subjugation, and exile.[1] Thus, the Hebrews in Egypt cried out to God to see them in their lowly servitude and rejoiced when God's might came to their rescue, as prayerfully remembered in liturgy:

> When the priest takes the basket from your hand and sets it down before the altar of the LORD your God, you shall make this response before the LORD your God: "A wandering Aramean was my ancestor; he went down into Egypt and lived there as an alien, few in number, and there he became a great nation, mighty and populous. When the Egyptians treated us harshly and afflicted us, by imposing hard labor on us, we cried to the LORD, the God of our ancestors; the LORD heard our voice and saw our affliction, our toil, and our oppression. The LORD brought us out of Egypt with a mighty hand and an outstretched arm, with a terrifying display of power, and

---

1. Stöger, "Humility," 385–86.

with signs and wonders; and he brought us into this place and gave us this land, a land flowing with milk and honey.[2]

The people came to believe in God's favor toward those who were lowly and insignificant, necessary for seeking divine favor before depending upon another's human strength or protection.

God favors the humble and powerless, often assisting them in overcoming the unrighteous proud and self-sufficient.[3] The heroine Judith, an unassuming widow who was divinely moved to take the life of the evil general Holofernes, cried out to the Lord, "For your strength does not depend on numbers, nor your might on the powerful. But you are the God of the lowly, helper of the oppressed, upholder of the weak, protector of the forsaken, savior of those without hope" (Jdt 9:11). Conversely, even those Hebrews of arrogant heart were subject to God's chastisement. The prophet Amos warned the people who had lost their sense of lowliness before God, "The Lord God has sworn by himself (says the LORD, the God of hosts): I abhor the pride of Jacob, and hate his strongholds; and I will deliver up the city and all that is in it" (Amos 6:8).

Those who sincerely desired God's mercy and assistance believed in the value of first recognizing their lowliness before God and expressing their felt wretchedness in penitential expressions of fasting and rending of garments, along with a heartfelt pursuit of divine forgiveness and moral conversion.[4] One's religious subjugation before God should be outwardly "lowly" (also described as "poor") while being interiorly aware of one's utter dependence upon God, confident upon divine providence for the needs of daily life.

This inner attitude had the potential to evoke one's sense of frailty and worthlessness before the overarching divine gaze which governs all human events, as Sirach instructed the scribe-in-training:

> The government of the earth is in the hand of the Lord,
> and over it he will raise up the right leader for the time . . .
> How can dust and ashes be proud? Even in life the human body decays.

---

2. Deut 26:4–9.

3. The Old Testament sages had notably more to say of pride than humility, containing admonitions such as "The LORD tears down the house of the proud, but maintains the widow's boundaries" (Prov 15:25); "All those who are arrogant are an abomination to the LORD; be assured, they will not go unpunished" (Prov 16:5); "Pride goes before destruction, and a haughty spirit before a fall" (Prov 16:18).

4. Stöger, "Humility," 386.

> A long illness baffles the physician; the king of today will die tomorrow.
> For when one is dead, he inherits maggots and vermin and worms.[5]

The fruits of humility were believed to include receiving divine favor for one's supplications and winning the respect of others.[6]

The New Testament

Among the synoptic Gospels, Luke presents especially well the importance of humility for life in the reign of God. The Lukan account focuses upon divine preference for the meek, the poor, the insignificant. God's plan of salvation occurs through a young virgin from an obscure village after she submits herself to the mysterious divine plan (Luke 1:26–38). Shortly afterward, Mary's *Magnificat* in the presence of her cousin is notably imbued with images underscoring the place of humility among the people of Israel (1:46–55). The widowed prophetess Anna, who spent night and day in humble prayer and fasting, recognizes the infant Jesus' special place in the life of Israel (2:36–38). The adult Jesus who identifies himself as "poor and humble of heart" teaches his disciples of God's special preference for the poor in parables such as that of the self-justified tax collector and the humble publican (18:9–14); the final justification of the poor Lazarus and the chastisement of the rich man after their deaths (16:19–31); and the restoration of the hemorrhaging woman who dares to touch him even though an outcast to her people (8:43–48). The greatest in the reign of God will be the least, those who prefer to live as insignificantly as children with no social standing or importance (9:46–48).

The Johannine Gospel points to humility as a key ingredient of Jesus' instruction to his disciples. As their teacher, Jesus incongruously washes their feet during the last supper, such a menial and humiliating a servant's task normally done by unclean foreigners. Just as God revealed the divine love through the incarnation, just as the Son of God would ultimately undergo his humiliating passion and death, so should the disciples be ready to serve the most menial needs among the least of their brothers and sisters.[7]

Pauline theology recognized Jesus, in his acceptance of human existence without regard for his divinity for the redemption of humankind, as

---

5. Sir 10:4; 9–11.
6. Stöger, "Humility," 387.
7. Stöger, "Humility," 390.

the quintessential model of humility. The "humiliations" of his incarnation and in his association with outsiders were the means by which Jesus glorified his heavenly Father, ultimately made known in accepting his unjust passion and death leading to his glorified resurrection. Through Jesus's attitude of vulnerability and trust in the Father's love was weakness made strong, through which the divine light overcame the shadows of despair and death.

The Pauline writings particularly exhorted the early Christians to the equivalent of humility, modesty, or freedom from personal vain ambition and pretentiousness, in service to their communion of fraternal charity.[8] Their means was through following the example of Jesus' lived *kenosis*, his self-emptying of any personal gain for the sake of others. Paul also exhorted Christians to recognize that individual gifts and abilities come from God, not to glorify oneself but rather for promoting God's glory and the good of the community:

> For by the grace given to me I say to everyone among you not to think of yourself more highly than you ought to think . . . For as in one body we have many members, and not all the members have the same function, so we, who are many, are one body in Christ, and individually we are members one of another.[9]

The Christian practice of humility can lead one to seek the good of others even at great personal cost:

> Bless those who persecute you; bless and do not curse them. Rejoice with those who rejoice, weep with those who weep. Live in harmony with one another; do not be haughty, but associate with the lowly; do not claim to be wiser than you are.[10]

The pastoral first letter of Peter, considered by many scholars to contain a baptismal instruction for converts (2:11—3:17), exhorts the listening community to observe blameless conduct with the aim of offering credible witness to the non-believers through maintaining "unity of spirit, sympathy, love for one another, a tender heart, and a humble mind" (3:8). The community elders, in their responsibility for the congregation, were instructed to serve "not for sordid gain but eagerly. Do not lord it over those in your charge but be examples to the flock" (5:2b), while the younger

---

8. See Adnés, "Humilité," 1148.
9. Rom 12:3–5.
10. Rom 12:14–16.

members likewise should accept their authority; and "all of you must clothe yourselves with humility in your dealings with one another, for 'God opposes the proud, but gives grace to the humble'" in the confidence that God may exalt them "in due time" (5:5b–6).

To summarize this section, we find that the practice of humility by the end of the first Christian century contains the Hebrew belief in God's preference for those who recognize their dependance upon divine providence for their needs. Jesus carried this attitude throughout his ministerial life in his filial love and regard for his heavenly Father and his self-giving for the sake of others. The post-resurrection followers of Jesus began to embrace these qualities both in imitation of their teacher as well as for the good of building up the Christian community, as testimony to the power of divine love in the surrounding world.

Humility in the Patristic Era

The Church Fathers

By the end of the first century, influential Christian writings encouraged the practice of humility among Christian disciples, in imitation of Jesus' lifelong humility. Humility's fruitfulness would show itself in fraternal unity within the growing number of Christian communities in the midst of cultural and social challenges.

The first-century bishop Clement of Rome wrote to the church of Corinth in the wake of ecclesial rebellion that challenged the legitimate church authority. His letter contains numerous appeals to the offending members, urging them to seek forgiveness from the community and their submission to its authority. We find in this pastoral letter at least three significant reasons for seeking humility in Christian life: followers of Jesus should seek to glorify their heavenly Father rather than any self-aggrandizement; exercising humble obedience to God's will and authority offered the best way to please and glorify God, following the examples of Abraham, Job, and David, and especially the example of Jesus's self-abasement before his Father. Also, the self-denial and abasement of humility form a disciple's privileged visible expression of God's love to other members in the church community and a support to its cohesion, giving evidence of Christ's presence within it.[11]

---

11. 1 Clem. chapters 16–18; 28; 38.

Ignatius of Antioch is traditionally recognized as the author of seven letters to Christian communities along his journey to execution in Rome. One finds within that Ignatius repeatedly exhorted the churches to unity with their local bishop as a sign of the unity between God and the church.[12] Ignatius also saw the value of cultivating Jesus' humility as a means to reveal the divine love among the nonbelievers and persecutors.

> But pray unceasingly ... for they offer ground for hoping that they may be converted and win their way to God. Give them an opportunity therefore, at least by your conduct, of becoming your disciples. Meet their angry outbursts with your own gentleness, their boastfulness with your humility, their reviling with your prayers ... their harshness with your meekness; and beware of trying to match their example ... let us strive to follow the Lord's example and see who can suffer greater wrong, who more deprivation, who more contempt.[13]

Origen of Alexandria (185–253), in his extensive apologetic work *Against Celsus*, gives an admirable defense of Christian practices in the face of pagan calumny and misinformation. At one point, he addresses Celsus's apparent misunderstanding of Christian humility as an inferior and insincere version of what had been counseled by ancient Greek philosophers. After informing Celsus that the practice of Christian humility was to be found in ancient Jewish practice, considerably older than the thought of Plato, Origen notes of Christian humility:

> Now these words show that he who is of humble mind does not by any means humble himself in an unseemly or inauspicious manner, falling down upon his knees, or casting himself headlong on the ground, putting on the dress of the miserable, or sprinkling himself with dust. But he who is of humble mind in the sense of the prophet, while walking in great and wonderful things, which are above his capacity—*viz.*, those doctrines that are truly great, and those thoughts that are wonderful—humbles himself under the mighty hand of God.[14]

Those people who follow the Christian practice are imitating no mere earthly philosopher, for they commit themselves to God through following the example of Jesus.

---

12. For examples, see Ign. *Eph.* 4 or Ign. *Phil.*
13. Ign. *Eph.* 10.
14. Origen, *Cels.* 6.15.

> [They place themselves] not under any one at random, but under the mighty hand of God, through Jesus Christ, the teacher of such instruction, who did not deem equality with God a thing to be eagerly clung to, but made Himself of no reputation, and took on Him the form of a servant, and being found in fashion as a man, humbled Himself, and became obedient unto death, even the death of the cross. And so great is this doctrine of humiliation, that it has no ordinary individual as its teacher; but our great Saviour Himself says: Learn of Me, for I am meek and lowly of heart, and you shall find rest for your souls.[15]

John Chrysostom (d. 407) possessed a very high regard for ordained ministry, and it was only through coercion that he accepted ordination as priest and bishop.[16] He was among the first in a line of patristic writers who considered humility as an essential quality for one accepting such a lofty vocation; for Chrysostom, humility was "mother, and root, and nurse, and foundation, and bond of all good things: without this we are abominable, and execrable."[17] He wrote that bishops in their preaching ministry should be indifferent to the praise of others; the efforts of even a well-prepared preacher otherwise would be for naught.[18]

In John's sermon on Jesus' parable of the Pharisee and the tax collector (Luke 18:9–14), Chrysostom underscores the foundational value of humility for growth in all other virtue and for vanquishing pride, always a stumbling-stone to growth in holiness. One product of this type of humility is the ability to admit our sinfulness, as he notes elsewhere:

> Even if we should have mounted to the very pinnacle of virtue, let us consider ourselves last of all; having learned that pride is able to cast down even from the heavens themselves him who takes not heed, and humbleness of mind to bear up on high from, the very abyss of sins him who knows how to be sober. For this it was that placed the publican before the Pharisee; whereas that, pride I mean and an overweening spirit, surpassed even an incorporeal power, that of the devil; while humbleness of mind and the

---

15. Origen, *Cels.* 6.15.

16. In Chrysostom's time, men with a reputation for holiness (notably monks) were sometimes coerced and even physically forced to accept ordination.

17. Chrysostom, *Hom. Act.*

18. Chrysostom, *Sac.* 5.3–4.

acknowledgment of his own sins committed brought the robber into Paradise before the Apostles.[19]

Lacking humility, all is futile. Indeed, it is also essential for the cultivation of wisdom:

> For humbleness of mind is the foundation of the love of wisdom which pertains to us. Even if thou shouldest have built a superstructure of things innumerable; even if almsgiving, even if prayers, even if fastings, even if all virtue; unless this have first been laid as a foundation, all will be built upon it to no purpose and in vain; and it will fall down easily, like that building which had been placed on the sand. For there is no one, no one of our good deeds, which does not need this; there is no one which separate from this will be able to stand.[20]

Augustine of Hippo (354–430) also regarded humility as a "practical" virtue, one that may be refined through a combination of divine grace and its daily practice as a part of Christian asceticism. Augustine held that practical humility contained three characteristics: Humility moves the one practicing the virtue to acknowledge personal weakness and sinfulness; it is recognition that God is the source of all blessing or ability to do good; and humility is a renouncement of self-will and submission of oneself to God as our divine creator.[21] For Augustine, Jesus was the "Doctor of Humility" who exercised it in every event of his life, evident in the incarnation, his lowly birth, his personal submission to John's baptism, and ultimately in his ignoble passion and death.[22]

Augustine notably encouraged clerical humility for bishops and presbyters since they enjoyed a number of special social privileges, such as exemption from imperial taxes and certain civic duties, and others that could be economically beneficial. Temptations to realize worldly honors and personal gain accompanied clerical life and Augustine urged them to remember that they ultimately would have to answer for their earthly conduct. In a letter to a neighboring bishop who was being pressured by others to rebaptize an individual, an action that would appease others but run contrary to the true apostolic faith, Augustine wrote:

---

19. Chrysostom, *Prof. evang.* 2.
20. Chrysostom, *Prof. evang.* 2.
21. Baasten, "Humility and Modern Ethics," 233–34.
22. Bacchi, "Ministry Characterized," 409.

> If, however, you do not rebaptize, seize the freedom of Christ, brother Maximinus; seize it, I beg you. In the sight of Christ do not fear the reproach or do not be terrified at the power of any human being. The honor of this world is passing; its pride is passing. In Christ's future judgement neither pulpits with flights of steps nor thrones with canopies nor flocks of processing and chanting nuns will be called to our defense . . . Those things which are here honors will there be burdens; those things which here buoy us up will then pull us down.[23]

Primitive and Early Monasticism

The monastic tradition, with roots reaching back to the third-century desert regions of North Africa, Palestine, and Syria, was a fertile source of wisdom and influence on early Christian humility. *The Sayings of the Desert Fathers* offers a rich source of monastic respect for the disposition of humility as a prerequisite for developing other virtues, and its importance for imitating the life of Christ. Anthony of Egypt (251–356), such an influential figure in both Eastern and Western Christian monasticism and its renowned teacher, counseled:

> What made our Lord Jesus Christ lay aside his garments, gird himself with a towel, and, pouring water into a basin, begin to wash the feet of those who were below Him (John 13:4, etc.), if not to teach us humility? For it was humility He showed us by example of what He then did. And indeed those who want to be accepted into the foremost rank cannot achieve this otherwise than through humility; for in the beginning the thing that caused downfall from heaven was a movement of pride. So, if a man lacks extreme humility, if he is not humble with all his heart, all his mind, all his spirit, all his soul and body—he will not inherit the kingdom of God.[24]

Recognizing one's faults and above all one's sinfulness, considering oneself as lower than one's fellow monks, an attitude of continual prayer, and bearing the daily burden of manual work were the ways to growth in monastic humility.

John Cassian spent several years learning from Eastern monastic masters and brought his accumulated knowledge to the West. He echoed the

---

23. Augustine, *Maxim.* 3.
24. Kadloubovsky and Palmer, *Early Fathers from the Philokalia*, 45–46.

Eastern tradition in underscoring the fundamental importance of humility in a monk's life, that of counteracting the often subtle but dangerous and corrosive quality of pride, as the way to regain the inner peace and joy that were lost due to sin. We find in Cassian's *Institutes* a list of signs indicating that humility was developing in the life of a monk; he offers ten of them situated within the context of monastic life. It is instructive to note a few basic points: A monk should be willing to disclose his thoughts and struggles to his spiritual *abba* (akin to a spiritual director); he should not trust in his own opinion; he should strive to maintain in his life the qualities of obedience, gentleness, and patience; and he should consider himself as inferior to all others in the community.[25]

By the close of the patristic era, appreciation for Christian humility was still rooted in the Old Testament, brought to perfection by the lifelong humility of Jesus, and considered an essential counsel to his disciples. Practicing selfless humility in the service of church unity and cohesion was seen as a particular imitation of Jesus by which one could offer an expression of unselfish love to God. Humility became considered an essential interior quality for those who wished to cultivate other virtues in the pursuit of divine wisdom. It was also counseled vigorously to those who exercised public leadership and ministry, becoming a perennial exhortation to clergy in future moments of church reform.

Humility in the Medieval Era

Medieval Christian Monasticism

From the sixth through twelfth centuries, monasticism was the principal locus of development in Christian spirituality. The monastic rule of Benedict of Nursia contains twelve progressive steps for a monk to practice on the way to mature humility. Benedict appreciated humility as a fundamental virtue for pursuing monastic holiness through obediently following his rule in daily life; the Benedictine pursuit of monastic humility was thus part of an overall ascetical program leading to community discipline and harmony.[26] This rule for cenobitic (conventual) monastic life eventually supplanted all other rules for Western monastic communities.

---

25. Cassian, *Inst.* 4.39.
26. RB 7.

The twelfth-century monastic regard for humility as foundational for monastic life was perhaps best articulated in the writings of the Cistercian Bernard of Clairvaux. Supported by earlier scriptural sources, Augustine, and the monastic tradition, Bernard has deeply affected the tradition of Christian spiritual life. He considered humility as necessary for growth in all virtue and Christian holiness. Bernard understood the importance of the incarnation as the Savior's humble abasement that enabled him to gain our redemption through his lifelong attitude of humility.[27] Growth in Christian holiness is a neverending pursuit; to do this, one must recognize one's innate tendency to sin. This attainment of self-awareness is the first step to growth in humility; to recognize and admit the truth about the self.

Whereas that nemesis of humility, pride, is our inordinate love of our excellence, Bernard's program taught that humility is "contempt for our excellence" that one gains through self-knowledge of one's sinfulness. Growth in humility, for Bernard, requires the monk to focus on his lack of holiness and imperfections rather than whatever inner excellence he may have attained:

> When a man thus takes stock of himself in the clear light of truth, he will discover that he lives in a region where likeness to God has been forfeited, and groaning from the depths of a misery to which he can no longer remain blind, will he not cry out to the Lord as the Prophet did: "In your truth you have humbled me"? How can he escape being genuinely humbled on acquiring this true self-knowledge, on seeing the burden of sin that he carries, the oppressive weight of his mortal body, the complexities of earthly cares, the corrupting influences of sensual desires; on seeing his blindness, his worldliness, his weakness, his embroilment in repeated errors; . . . one to whom vice is welcome, virtue repugnant?[28]

Bernard gave considerable attention to the antithetical relationship between humility and pride. His work, *The Degrees of Humility and Pride*, offers twelve steps through which growth in spiritual pride gradually returns a monk to carelessness or indifference to sin. Its remedy is adherence to a complementary list of twelve steps of humility, to be pursued throughout a monk's life in common with his confreres. Bernard also simplified the degrees of humility by reducing them to three basic grades: sufficient

---

27. Sermon 42, verses 6–7. See Bernard of Clairvaux, "Sermon 42," 214–15.

28. Sermon 36 (on the Canticle of Canticles), verse 4. See Bernard of Clairvaux, "Sermon 36," 178.

humility (to subject oneself to superiors and not to prefer oneself over others); abundant humility (to subject oneself to one's equals and not to prefer oneself to one's inferiors); and superabundant humility (to subject oneself to one's inferiors).[29]

The Medieval Quest to Follow in the Footsteps of Jesus

Priestly and episcopal ministry suffered between the ninth and thirteenth centuries as a result of the excessive influences of both royalty and rich patrons upon both monastic and diocesan church life. There developed among the clergy a virtual split between "higher" and "lower" clergy; the former enjoyed much prestige and power as a result of its proximity to the upper ruling classes, while the lower clergy typically were left to minister and survive as best they could among the rural and illiterate. Ordained ministry among the higher clergy came to be identified with social recognition, privilege, and financial gain, giving to ordained ministry an existence that was perceived by many as too removed from the life example of Jesus. This attitude led to a growing popular exhortation for humility in Church ministers through the various forms of mendicant common life that emerged during this period, most notably within the various lay *humiliati* movements and the emergence of the Franciscan, canons regular, and Dominican forms of consecrated life, that sought to follow a life more in tune with humility and dependence on divine providence. A principal desire of reformers during this time was to restore in preachers a more credible and visible example of the so-called "apostolic life," the idealized evangelical lifestyle and practice of Jesus and the Twelve. Anxious for the restoration of ecclesiastical holiness, reformers also sought to return the church to a meeker state—to become divested of property and riches for the sake of a greater expression of humility and dependence on God in the midst of a power-conscious and politically-minded monarchical society.

The scholastic theological systematization of humility and other virtues had an enduring impact on subsequent Christian theology and spirituality through the twentieth century, affecting how virtues were later understood in relationship to the person, moral life, and one's relationship to God. Early on, however, it sparked a reaction on the part of other masters of the Christian spiritual life, notably in the work of Bonaventure (1221–74), who stressed the experiential dimension of theology over the

---

29. Aumann, *Spiritual Theology*, 302.

scholastic approach that they considered as lifeless and too estranged from practical Christian spiritual life.

Due partly to this reaction against scholastic formalization, the fourteenth century greatly influenced the Christian understanding and appreciation for humility through the popular writing *The Imitation of Christ*. The work recalls sincere followers of Jesus to earnest prayer, humble submission to God, and otherwise to consider oneself of no account among God's creatures:

> There is no lesson so profound or so useful as this lesson of self-knowledge and of self-contempt. Claim nothing for yourself, think of others kindly and with admiration; that is the height of wisdom, and its masterpiece. Never think yourself better than the next man, however glaring his faults, however grievous his offences; your are in good dispositions now, but how long will they last? Tell yourself, "We are frail, all of us, but none so frail as I."[30]

Though apparently written within a monastic-like setting and intended to inject some of its spirituality into the wider world, this work became a tremendous influence on lay, consecrated religious, and priestly spiritual life through the mid-twentieth century and was popular reading in religious life communities. Unfortunately, a superficial reading without considering the historical context and other concerns of fourteenth-century spiritual writers can lead some contemporary readers to cultivate an imbalanced perception of one's sinfulness and need to practice exaggerated acts of humility, or "humiliations." Consider another quote from the *Imitation*:

> You that are but earth and slime, learn how to humble yourself, to bow down beneath the feet of all. Learn how to break your own will and to surrender yourself in complete submission.[31]

> Direct the fire of your anger against yourself; do not let pride, that monstrous growth, draw nourishment from you any more; but show yourself so submissive, so unimportant, that everyone may walk over you, trample you like mud in the streets. And if they do, what reason have you to complain, you worthless man?[32]

We can make some observations about the understanding of humility by the close of the medieval period. The practical appreciation for humility

---

30. à Kempis, *Imitation* 1.2.
31. à Kempis, *Imitation* 3.13.
32. à Kempis, *Imitation* 3.13.

was heavily influenced by monastic life. While promoting the life example of Jesus as salutary for Christian disciples, monastic humility was regarded as essential for growth in obedience and overall function of organized religious communities. There was also a growing emphasis and merit attached to practices of humiliations, acts of humbling oneself before God and God as represented in others; in time, this will have both positive and negative effects upon later Christian practices of humility, notably within consecrated religious institutes.

Humility in the Modern Era

Roman Catholic Counter-reform

Just prior to the Council of Trent, the formation of numerous "societies of clerics regular," such as the Society of Jesus, gave notable focus on the practice of humility. The founder of the Jesuits, Ignatius of Loyola (1491–1556), composed his *Spiritual Exercises* as a discernment instrument for those who desired to join his religious congregation in service to the church's emerging foreign missionary efforts. The *Exercises* regarded humility as necessary for one's observing the Jesuit vow of obedience, so central to their life and mission. The text presented three ascending grades of practiced humility to consider in making their discernment. The lowest, necessary for one's salvation and thus obligatory for all, was to obey every law of God under any circumstances or danger. The person who sought to reach the second and more complete expression of humility would strive to avoid committing even the least venial sin. Finally, the greatest expression was for the exercitant to observe not only the first two, but also desire to more fully live the life of Jesus Christ by choosing poverty rather than wealth, being despised as Christ over personal honors, and be considered as worthless and a fool for Christ.[33] These three degrees of practiced humility would prove influential upon subsequent lay and consecrated religious spirituality, societies of clerics regular, and secular priestly formation.

In France, Pierre Cardinal de Bérulle (1575–1629) sought to implement the pastoral and clerical reforms that emerged from the Council of Trent. He was particularly interested to restore appreciation for the awesomeness and dignity of God through reviving Christian piety and humble devotion to Jesus, a perspective that he felt had been considerably eroded by the earlier

---

33. Ignatius of Loyola, *Spiritual Exercises* 165–67.

Renaissance exaltation of the human person. Bérulle's thought found a more enduring effect in the seventeenth-century efforts of his most influential disciple, Jean-Jacques Olier. Olier taught in his *Introduction to the Christian Life and Virtues* that disciples should glorify God through adopting Jesus' virtue of religion, the core of which was his desire to give every bit of himself in an offering to his heavenly father. Fundamental to this was the need to accept and follow Jesus' life example of humility, the way of self-denial, so to further the work of redemption through the centuries:

> Humility has three parts. The first is to take pleasure in self-knowledge . . . to know and to love one's own vileness and misery . . . If the soul is humble, it should love the vileness to which it is reduced through sin, but should despise its sin inasmuch as it is opposed to God . . . We should not only consider [Jesus] in the humiliations that he bore himself . . . but also in the humiliations and the scorn he desires to suffer in his Mystical Body and in his members.[34]

Anglican Spirituality

Anglican Reformation religious texts that encouraged humility were still circulating in the nineteenth-century English-speaking world and propagated through English theologians and religious preachers of the early modern era. This understanding of humility, widely considered as an essential Christian virtue that fostered a challenging personal asceticism for its followers, drew from *The Imitation of Christ* that was popular in England. Christian preaching and religious instruction of the time encouraged personal manifestations of humility as safeguards against the vice of pride, considered as the original sin of the devil and the root of all other sins.

Signs of pride's malevolent presence in seventeenth-century class-conscious England included any thoughts, attitudes, or emotions resulting from any personal desire for improving social status and accumulating power. One's cultivation of "true" humility, on the contrary, would be evident in two principal areas: a pervasive regard for oneself as an unworthy individual that should pervade all of one's existence, and an easy acceptance of others' lowly regard of oneself.[35] The bishop-theologian Jeremy Taylor (1613–67) praised humility as "the great ornament and jewel of Christian

---

34. Thompson, *Bérulle and the French School*, 233–35.
35. Konkola, "Have We Lost Humility?," 187.

religion; that whereby it is distinguished from all the wisdom of the world; it not having been taught by the wise men of the Gentiles, but first put into a discipline, and made part of a religion, by our Lord Jesus Christ."[36] The principal attitudes to cultivate were self-distrust and considering oneself as lower in dignity than others. In Taylor's work, *The Rule and Exercise of Holy Living*, one of his seventeen observations of humility counsels that:

> Humility consists not in railing against thyself, or wearing mean clothes, or going softly and submissively; but in hearty and real evil or mean opinion of thyself. Believe thyself an unworthy person heartily, as thou believest thyself to be hungry, or poor, or sick, when thou art so.[37]

The virtue of humility toward the close of the Modern Era, while still basically rooted in its earliest spiritual understandings, had become significantly influenced by concerns within monastic and clerical life from the later medieval period. It had developed, however, an even sharper focus on the need to vanquish any trace of interior pride. Again, the remedy for this was to adopt Jesus' attitude of humility, notably through enduring whatever daily personal *humiliations* that may arise. The disciple was to accept humiliations both in imitation of Jesus who suffered the humiliations of his life, passion and death. Shouldering one's daily humiliations also offered a way to extend Christ's redemptive suffering into the present day.

II. TOWARDS A CONTEMPORARY APPRECIATION FOR CHRISTIAN HUMILITY

Humility, an Orphaned Virtue

The practice of humility finds little encouragement within the political and economic spheres of western society, notably within the United States. The American self-image that values personal sufficiency while recalling familiar individuals who have "pulled themselves up by their bootstraps" to achieve a rewarding life is central to the American success story, and American history revels in the stories of financial tycoons and successful inventors who dared to take bold risks that helped to produce their fortunes. Nor do Americans particularly value political leaders who might describe

---

36. Taylor, *Rule and Exercise* 2.4, 4–3.
37. Taylor, *Rule and Exercise* 2.4.3, 4–3.

themselves as humble, preferring that they are able to take initiative and act boldly when necessary in both domestic and international diplomacy.

Several significant factors have mitigated the contemporary appreciation for authentic Christian humility. One reason is the loss of a balanced Christian understanding due to past exaggerations. A popular image of a humble person is of a "human doormat" individual who passively allows others to psychologically walk over him or her, refusing to stand up to stronger personalities in a misguided sense of humility. Another misrepresentation would be the case of a psychologically abused woman and mother who is counseled to remain in what could well be a physically threatening marriage while drawing support from images of a silent, suffering, and "humble" Jesus. These examples alone would deter most people from considering the virtue of Christian humility as something worthwhile.

A perusal of contemporary Christian theological dictionaries and encyclopedias reveals that humility as a virtue is mostly overlooked in contemporary Western Christian theology.[38] This may be in part due to recent studies identifying the abuse of imposed humility in maintaining control over others, whether culturally, politically, or even within Christian church structures. Several Christian feminist theologians have sought to recover an alternative understanding of humility than what has been historically understood, seeking to rehabilitate the word from a male perspective that has emphasized humble subservience and obedience as bulwarks against pride. One author wrote:

> Concepts of "sin as pride" and humility will continue to be subject to distortion if humility is only falsely seen as a response to pride and viewed from the perspective and stories of the elite and the powerful (intellectuals, academics, politicians, religious leaders, and so on). Genuine humility must be seen as a voluntary act, never mistakenly viewed as a "naturally occurring" obligation. Genuine humility should not be imposed on others by the privileged and the powerful but should be understood as the means of empowering individual selves to be part of a larger "we."[39]

Properly-understood Christian humility still has a place for our contemporary day and in Western culture that disregards the virtue at its peril. A theologically-sound sense of humility has an essential place in one's relationship with God through Jesus Christ, with one's brothers and sisters in

38. For one survey, see Konkola, "Have We Lost Humility?," 190–200.
39. Hinson-Hasty, "Revisiting Feminist Discussions of Sin," 114.

Christ, and in one's relationship with the rest of creation. Selling humility in the present day, however, calls for a more nuanced understanding of both humility and pride.

Authentic Christian Humility as a Check against Pride

Contemporary humility enjoys a range of applications that we may judge as either true or false. Living under the dictates of false humility by denying one's personal worth or giftedness can result from prior psychological or physical abuse, or other personal trauma. One may learn to use false humility in one's life, or perhaps impose it upon another, as a way to gaining sympathy or even to emotionally control them. True humility does not exhibit itself in what may be called "self-loss" that results from one's loss of self-worth in a marriage or other personal relationship or through other social conditioning. To the contrary, true Christian humility is the result of honest self-appraisal and awareness of one's gifts and talents as well as weaknesses and sinful tendencies, not far from the apostle Paul's exhortation in Romans 12:3: "I say to everyone among you not to think of yourself more highly than you ought to think, but to think with sober judgement, each according to the measure of faith that God has assigned."

Pride in contemporary thought likewise bears a range of understandings, whether rooted in one's personal selfishness, self-confidence, or self-esteem. One succinct Christian definition considers pride as "an irreligious and antisocial assertion of the self."[40] Note that we are not speaking merely of self-assertion, rather an inordinate self-assertion that is exaggerated to the point where pride becomes indifferent and injurious to one's relationship with God and others. This is the understanding of what may be called "sinful pride" as opposed to those emotionally transient feelings of what we may label as "legitimate pride"—for example, the pride of parents for having raised loving and happy children, or the justifiable pride of an author who has produced a best-selling book after much effort. Sinful pride will express itself in such ways as excessive personal vanity, conceit, self-contempt, self-pity, and ultimately will prove destructive in the lives of individuals and their relationships with others. For good reason, sinful pride has been considered from medieval times as one of the seven capital sins.

---

40. The article by Paul Sands was very helpful for proposing this contemporary view of pride and humility. Sands, "Deadly Sin of Pride," 40–49.

The 1994 *Catechism of the Catholic Church* underscores the traditional belief that pride is a capital sin (no. 1866) and the root of envy; its remedy is for the disciple to live with an attitude of continual humility (2540). The document also notes that humility has an irreplaceable place within Christian prayer: Humility is the root of Christian prayer (2559); it enhances our adoration of God (2628); humility incites our desire for forgiveness of sin (2631); and it purifies our desire to follow divine prompting and receive spiritual gifts (2706, 2713). The *Catechism* exhorts Christian disciples to practice lifelong humility since it was part of Jesus' life from his birth; it is also a necessity for life in the Reign of God (525–26). Indeed, humility that embodies our dependence upon God for our needs is an essential quality for disciples helping to establish this reign:

> How will Jerusalem welcome her Messiah? Although Jesus had always refused popular attempts to make him king, he chooses the time and prepares the details for his messianic entry into the city of "his father David." . . . Jesus conquers the Daughter of Zion, a figure of his Church, neither by ruse nor by violence, but by the humility that bears witness to the truth. And so the subjects of his kingdom on that day are children and God's poor, who acclaim him as had the angels when they announced him to the shepherds.[41]

Christian Humility in Relationships with God, with Others, and as Part of Creation

Christian regard for humility addresses, most fundamentally, one's personal stance before God. A personal life guided by humility will have consequences beyond this core relationship: It will extend outward and be evident in one's relationship with other people and, even further, it will impact one's self-understanding as a created being, coexisting with the rest of creation.

With God

In the depths of a disciple's heart, the person of Jesus Christ beckons to us as example and guide, the one whose entire life was an expression of humility.

---

41. *Catechism of the Catholic Church*, no. 559.

A man of his culture, Jesus embodied an attitude of humble reverence toward his heavenly Father through his submission to the Father's divine love. Jesus in his total dependence on this love was interiorly free of self-concern, free to simply follow the Father's mysterious plan for his salvific role. Jesus was the expression *par excellence* of both the poor and lowly *anawim* of Israel and the suffering servant of Isaiah who relied on divine providence for their needs. Jesus' lifelong dependence upon the Father's love allowed him to be totally free for ministry to others as both son of God and brother to all. His life sought no self-serving honors; rather, he came into the world only to make visible the depth of the Father's love for us and Jesus' love for the Father that, ultimately, would consume his earthly life.

Jesus' life example points to his heavenly father as the ultimate source of every blessing, every breath, everything that we receive. We receive all of this freely from God's love for us, and there is no material thing we can imagine, however precious, with which to compensate that fathomless generosity. The only thing we are asked is to love one another in grateful response. In the end, *all* is gift, for us to receive with gratitude.

With Others

The inner freedom and gratitude that Jesus enjoyed allowed him to relate to others with no impulse to "lord it over" them, but rather with an attitude that respected the dignity of all people who shared the same heavenly father.

To the degree that we exalt ourselves over others, we tend to isolate ourselves from them and seek to buttress our self-esteem by comparing ourselves to one another. This attitude runs the risk of hardening the distinctions among people according to nationality, race, gender, sexual orientation, religion, or even in dividing Christian disciples into groups of "clerical" and "lay." Such self-imposed isolation is damaging for several reasons. It obscures the vision of the reign of God on earth that does not hold to such distinctions, in which we no longer will seek to dominate over others because of any limiting self-identification. Living this way can also inhibit the revelation of truth that is offered to us through the lives and experiences of our brothers and sisters, children of the same Creator.

Growth in personal humility reduces our desire to build walls or fences between us and others, allowing us to coexist with a liberated attitude of openness and approachability to one another, grateful for the gifts that other people bring to our lives rather than regarding them in some utilitarian view to serve our self-interest. We also grow in beholding one another as brothers and sisters in Christ, capable of revealing hidden facets of God to one another, and of our inescapable interdependence.

As Part of Creation

Our ability to see other people as sons and daughters of the same Father leads us to honor each person as a unique gift to one another, each with the potential of being a channel of God's grace and love. Our gratitude to God for other people as channels of grace can also challenge us to receive *all* of creation as divine gift. This will affect our underlying attitude toward the created world. Do we consider creation as something to be used as we see fit, guided by a reckless sense of dominance over it? Or, can we imagine a more integral view of creation as gift, one that will lead us to identify and change unreflective habits of abusing or squandering it?

The Hebrew Scriptures reveal in many places that the people of God, especially the "people of the land," were primarily attuned to agricultural realities. They most likely beheld the gifts of nature and produce as divine gifts since productivity depended so much upon God's goodness. Their gratitude to God for the bounty of the earth sings forth here and there among the Psalms, as, for instance:

> You visit the earth and water it, you greatly enrich it;
> the river of God is full of water;
> you provide the people with grain, for so you have prepared it.
> You water its furrows abundantly, settling its ridges,
> softening it with showers, and blessing its growth . . .
> The meadows clothe themselves with flocks, the valleys deck themselves with grain,
> they shout and sing together for joy.[42]

The Old Testament also contains numerous examples where, through the eyes of faith, creation revealed God's care for them as well as God's might and grandeur. The Exodus saga alone reveals several such moments. God's compelling signs to Pharaoh that the Hebrew slaves should be allowed to leave their bondage, and their escape from the Egyptians through the parted Red Sea, both involve natural signs and wonders.

---

42. Ps 65:9–10; 13.

Humility and Grateful Living in the Reign of God

Jesus, born into the surrounding Jewish culture, would have shared this viewpoint; indeed he utilized created elements to effect his Father's will during his lifetime. Jesus made use of many agricultural parables in bringing others into right relationship with God such as the sowing of seed on good and rocky ground (Matt 13:5) and the foolish grain farmer who stored up an abundant grain harvest (Luke 12:15). His ministry, likewise, made free use of created matter. Lowly spittle mixed with dirt helped to give eyesight (John 9:6); abundant wine at the Cana wedding revealed the coming of the messianic kingdom (John 2); the simple sharing of bread and wine announced that Jesus' ministry would end in his death while revealing that he would be with them in a new way (John 13). Creation has, in other words, a *sacramental* quality, capable of revealing to us something of the divine mystery and glory through sensate matter.

The struggle to arrive at a responsible view of creation and the environment through the lens of a balanced Christian view of humanity is one concern of the papal encyclical *Laudato Si'*. In challenging a worldview that seeks to dominates creation and is driven by destructive technological and industrial presumptions, Pope Francis asserts that a more humility-based view of humanity is essential in order to halt the ecological damage caused by unjust equilateral domination:

> We are not God. The earth was here before us and it has been given to us . . . Although it is true that we Christians have at times incorrectly interpreted the Scriptures, nowadays we must forcefully reject the notion that our being created in God's image and given dominion over the earth justifies absolute domination over other creatures . . . Each community can take from the bounty of the earth whatever it needs for subsistence, but it also has the duty to protect the earth and to ensure its fruitfulness for coming generations.[43]

Such an attitude calls for life guided by humility. Christian humility models one's relationship with our heavenly creator through adopting the attitude of the son. It allows us to regard other persons as unique gifts for whom we share responsibility. Humility also can lead us to cultivate a grateful respect for the gift of all material creation in which we coexist with an attitude of stewardship for the sake of future generations.

All of creation, including humanity, has the sacramental potential to reveal the love and wonders of our God to those with eyes to see, ears to hear, and a grateful humility to accept.

---

43. Francis, *Laudato Si'*, no. 67.

3

Christian Obedience to the Authority of Christ

OBEDIENCE TODAY MAY LESS likely be considered as a virtue than a necessary evil for living in a civilized society. Contemporary Western society tends to place a premium on autonomy, affording the maximum freedom to do as the individual pleases. This attitude differs from the Christian sense of freedom as the personal condition that enables one to be free and unfettered in discerning and responding to the divine movements of the Holy Spirit through "listening intently" for the divine voice in one's life (in Latin, *ob-audire*).

The earliest Christian understanding of practicing obedience was through interiorizing the virtues and teachings of Jesus in what is called his filial obedience to the Father. Soon, however, it grew to include the obligation to obey spiritual superiors in positions of authority, recognized as representatives of divine authority. Secular leaders (e.g., emperors and kings) also merited respect as individuals who received their mandate of authority from God, the source of all authority. Obedience to authority of one's superiors gradually became the principal means to practice the virtue.

Christian Obedience to the Authority of Christ

I. CHRISTIAN OBEDIENCE THROUGH THE CENTURIES

In Scriptures

The Old Testament

At the heart of the Old Testament we find the long history of salvation, and the struggle for God's people to live their covenant relationship with God. God is the divine creator, while humanity exists among God's dependent creatures who live and die by God's permitting it. The Hebrew Scripture contains God's self-revelation to God's people, calling them to accept God as the only true source of their salvation and acknowledge this faith through their obedience to God, ultimately by observing the Jewish covenant and the law.[1]

The obedience of the Jewish people was fundamental to their relationship with God, seeking their greatest happiness through submitting themselves to the divinely-inspired word of both text and tradition. Literary examples are plentiful. Adam and Eve had enjoyed the bliss of God's blessings in paradise until they turned from obedience and ate from the fruit of the forbidden tree (Gen 3). Abram obeyed God's call to leave his homeland and security in return for divine blessings of greatness, land, and protection (Gen 12:1–3). Abram, having been renamed Abraham by God because of his faithful obedience, offered a gripping example of obedience in his willingness to sacrifice his only son Isaac, saved by God at the last minute and given the promise of even greater blessing (Gen 22:1–19). The Exodus story portrays Moses cooperating with God's plan to lead the Hebrews out of Egypt, though tragically losing his right to enter the promised land because of a disobedient act (Num 20:12).

Obedience to the law of the covenant, rooted in the Decalogue and elaborated in Deuteronomy, was the road to salvation and fullness of divine blessing:

> Happy are those
> who do not follow the advice of the wicked,
> or take the path that sinners tread, or sit in the seat of scoffers;
> but their delight is in the law of the LORD,
> and on his law they meditate day and night . . .
> In all that they do, they prosper.[2]

---

1. Johnson, "Old Testament Demand," 28–30.
2. Ps 1:1–3.

Worship of God in prayers, offerings, and songs are made acceptable by one's faithful response to God's will through observing the law:

> Sacrifice and offering you do not desire, but you have given me an open ear.
> Burnt offering and sin offering you have not required.
> Then I said, "Here I am;
> in the scroll of the book it is written of me.
> I delight to do your will, O my God;
> your law is within my heart.[3]

Time and time again, God's people fail in their observance of the law. Time and time again, God calls them to renew their covenant, finally promising them that they would soon enter into a new and more enduring one, indelibly impressed within their deepest selves:

> The days are surely coming, says the LORD, when I will make a new covenant with the house of Israel and the house of Judah . . . I will put my law within them, and I will write it on their hearts; and I will be their God and they shall be my people. No longer shall they teach one another, or say to each other, "Know the LORD," for they shall all know me, from the least of them to the greatest, says the LORD.[4]

The New Testament

Jesus revealed the way of life that fulfills this "new covenant." "My food is to do the will of him who sent me and to complete his work" (John 4:34) captures the essence of Jesus' earthly mission. A gospel account from his childhood mentions his growth in obedience to his parents after they found him in the temple with the elders and returned to Nazareth (Luke 2:51). Jesus' sojourn in the desert unveiled his adult vocation when he resisted three temptations to earthly greatness in order to faithfully observe and respond in obedience to the Father's commands (Luke 4:1–13). His entire life was guided by the fullness of love existing between him and his heavenly Father; this divine law of love, expressed imperfectly in the Jewish law that was impossible to completely fulfill, became visible and was manifested to the world through the person and example of Jesus. Through his encounters

---

3. Ps 40:6–8.
4. Jer 31:31–34.

with others and especially in his passion and crucifixion, Jesus taught that God's will for us is, simply, to "love one another as I have loved you" (John 15:12). Obedience to God, through following Jesus' example of living, led his disciples to exhibit that same love among others that Jesus shared with those around him.

For Paul, Jesus' attitude of obedience to the Father was the way through which he redeemed outcast humanity. Jesus was "born under the law, in order to redeem those who were under the law, so that we might receive adoption as children" (Gal 4:4–5). Just as the disobedient sin of Adam opened the way for evil and death to enter the world, Paul observed, the obedience of Jesus conquered sin and death (Rom 5:18–21). Faith is submission to the good news (Rom 1:5); those who acknowledge the obedience of Christ through their obedient submission to his salvific life example give glory to God (2 Cor 9:13).

The Pauline texts also speak of authority; that of God, Christ, and persons who are called to exercise a share in the divine authority. Echoing the Platonist hierarchical view of reality that prescribed respect to those in higher social and civil social realms, we find that Christians are called to obey civil authority since it derives its right to receive obedience from God in the service of good and not evil (Rom 13:1–4). Using the prevalent view found in both Jewish and pagan worlds, Paul also sees this as the natural order in one's spiritual relationship with God:

> I commend you because you remember me in everything and maintain the traditions just as I handed them on to you. But I want you to understand that Christ is the head of every man, and the husband is the head of his wife, and God is the head of Christ.[5]

At the end of the first century, early Christian obedience is understood as hearing God's invitation to salvation and responding to it by following the self-giving life example of Jesus. Obedience to church authority, however, has become a significant theme in some of the later first-century pastoral letters. Gone are the the original twelve apostles who had followed Jesus during his earthly ministry; Paul, likewise, has been dead for some forty years. The scattered Christian church centers are now beset by a host of other difficulties. Christians have been expelled from association with their ancestral Jewish religious life and are now discovering their own religious identity. Their disassociation from the Jewish religion is adding to

---

5. 1 Cor 11:3.

a strained relationship with the surrounding Jewish and pagan neighbors that is contributing to occasional bouts of Christian persecution. Influential strains of Greek philosophical belief and dualist Gnosticism are challenging the Christians' central belief in Jesus as the incarnate Son of God.[6] In the face of these obstacles, Christian church communities are moving toward a greater internal organization in which religious authority is based on its faithful transmission of what is called the "apostolic tradition," the body of teaching that was understood to be rooted in the ministry and preaching of Jesus, and handed down through the apostles. The heightened insistence on accepting ecclesiastical authority will have its effect on the subsequent understanding of Christian obedience.

Obedience in the Patristic Era

The Church Fathers

The letter of Pope Clement of Rome to the Corinthians exhorted the local church to respect their appointed leadership. Rome was gradually becoming regarded as a privileged seat of authority in the church, aided by the fact that the remains of the apostles Peter and Paul rested there. Clement's words, therefore, held no small significance among the other Christian bishops.

His letter begins by praising the community's previous harmony, the fruit of the members' rightly-ordered obedience:

> Indeed, was there ever a visitor in your midst that did not approve your excellent and steadfast faith? Or did not admire your discreet and thoughtful Christian piety? . . . You certainly did everything without an eye to rank or station in life, and regulated your conduct by God's commandments. You were submissive to your officials and paid the older men among you the respect due to them. The young you trained to habits of self-restraint and sedateness. The wives you enjoined to discharge all their duties with a conscience pure and undefiled, and to cherish a dutiful affection for their husbands; you taught them also to stay within the established

---

6. Religious movements of Gnosticism were spawned from the collision of Christianity with Greek philosophical thought; the latter, in general, placed a lower value upon material creation as inferior to higher and more spiritual realms. The most severe cases held that creation and the spiritual realm were locked in a perpetual struggle between evil and good.

norm of obedience in managing the household with decency and consummate prudence.[7]

In moving though somewhat lengthy prose, Clement makes a universal case for obedience in asserting that the rest of the created world exists in a harmonious coexistence through following the ways of God's plan for nature:

> The heavens revolve by His arrangement and are subject to Him in peace. Day and night complete the revolution ordained by Him, and neither interferes in the least with the other. Sun and moon and the starry choirs, obedient to His arrangement, roll on in harmony, without any deviation, through their appointed orbits. The earth bears fruit according to His will in its proper seasons, and yields the full amount of food required for men and beasts and all the living things on it, neither wavering nor altering any of His decrees... The basin of the boundless sea, firmly built by His creative act for the collecting of waters, does not burst the barriers set up all around it, and does precisely what has been assigned to it... The seasons—spring, summer, autumn, and winter—make room for one another in peaceful succession. The stations of the winds at the proper time render their service without disturbance. Ever-flowing springs, created for enjoyment and for health, without fail offer to men their life-sustaining breasts. The smallest of the animals meet in peaceful harmony. All these creatures the mighty Creator and Master of the universe ordained to act in peace and concord, thus benefitting the universe, but most abundantly ourselves who have taken refuge under His mercies through our Lord Jesus Christ; to whom be the glory and majesty forever and evermore. Amen.[8]

Clement believed that Christians were called to give obedience to God through following the teachings of Christ, re-presented to all generations through those appointed to positions of leadership:

> The Apostle preached to us the Gospel received from Jesus Christ, and Jesus Christ was God's Ambassador. Christ, in other words, comes with a message from God, and the Apostles with a message from Christ. Both these orderly arrangements, therefore, originate from the will of God. And so, after receiving their instructions and being fully assured through the Resurrection of our Lord Jesus

---

7. 1 Clem. 1.
8. 1 Clem. 20.

Christ, as well as confirmed in faith by the word of God, they went forth, equipped with the fullness of the Holy Spirit, to preach the good news that the Kingdom of God was close at hand. From land to land, accordingly, and from city to city they preached, and from among their earliest converts appointed men whom they had tested by the Spirit to act as bishops and deacons for the future believers.[9]

We find in this document the fundamental principles of apostolic succession and Christian church order: the transmission of God's saving plan for humanity through the teachings of Jesus and handed on to the Christian church by his appointed apostles and their legitimate apostolic descendants, thus providing a divinely-rooted lineage of authority.

Irenaeus of Lyons (d. 202) is celebrated for his lengthy arguments against several heretical gnostic movements. The fourth book in his major work *Against Heresies* instructs that Christ the son of God offers the way to salvation through following his life example and teaching. God's chosen people of the Old Testament responded to faith in God through obedience to the Law; our obedience through following the life example of Jesus offers the way to do so completely. The Word Incarnate gave a visible example of fullest glory rendered to the Father through his life of complete faithfulness:

> And for this reason did the Word become the dispenser of the paternal grace for the benefit of men . . . revealing God indeed to men, but presenting man to God . . . For the glory of God is a living man; and the life of man consists in beholding God. For if the manifestation of God which is made by means of the creation, affords life to all living in the earth, much more does that revelation of the Father which comes through the Word, give life to those who see God.[10]

The "living man" refers to Jesus. The Christian disciple seeks to realize the fullness of human life through union with the Father, by faithfully reproducing in oneself the faithful and obedient living example of the Son.[11]

An enhanced understanding of Christian obedience came from the earliest centuries and various works of the so-called "Apostolic Fathers" whose claim to authority was rooted in their association with the original

---

9. 1 Clem. 42.

10. Irenaeus, *Haer.* 4.20.7.

11. This Irenaean quote is the source of a misquoted yet popular contemporary phrase attributed to Irenaeus, "the glory of God is man fully alive" when speaking of individual personal development as a principal good; a more careful reading of the wider text gives a better sense of its context. See Reardon, "Man Alive," paras. 1–17.

apostles of Jesus. The church at this time had a tenuous organizational structure, more local than universal. That would begin to change with the emperor Constantine's Edict of Milan in 313 that legitimized Christianity, eventually leading to the adoption of Christianity as the official religion of the Roman empire. Following the example of the obedient Jesus would remain the kernel of the virtue, while observing the authority of religious and secular leaders grew to include honoring the inherent authority of one's "betters," those who occupied a higher social class than oneself.

Obedience in the the Medieval Era

Christian Monasticism

The early Christian monastic tradition placed a high value on the practice of obedience, especially with the advent of cenobitic or conventual communities living under one roof and answerable to an abbot or another representative. The first monastic solitaries had to contend with inner struggles to obey God's will by observing the commandments and persevering in the daily routine of personal prayer and manual work. Cenobitic monasticism, with a diversity of individuals living closely together according to a well-ordered program of life, relied on the practice of obedience to God's will as presented to them in a highly-structured communal monastic rule and through the mandates of their appointed superiors.

The first fourth-century rules for monastic communities provided means to test a prospective monk's will for signs of obstinance before being admitted as a member. Monks showing evidence of an unbending will might cling to the habits of their former lives and fail to adapt to the demands of their monastic rule. This testing sometimes included imposing severe exercises of humility (such as assigning them the most menial or arduous tasks) and occasionally issuing excessive demands of obedience by the superior, the responses to which were to be immediate, unquestioned, and without complaint. There are recorded stories in which monks were able to observe obedience even to the extent of denying one's basic human needs or even bonds of parenthood.[12]

---

12. Cassian, *Inst.* 4.24–29. The twenty-seventh chapter recalls one disturbing example in which, to test an aspiring monk's ability to detach himself from parental ties to his young son, the superior ordered the aspirant to throw his crying boy into a nearby river; fortunately, some fellow monks intervened and saved the child. Cassian, *Inst.* 4.27.

The sixth-century monastic rule of Benedict incorporates much of the thought and organization of earlier rules but with its own particular objectives and a more moderate tone. The rule places more emphasis on the cultivation of fraternal love than on ascetical practices (though these are not absent) and considers organization, authority, and obedience in the light of cultivating the love of Christ in the community. The first few sentences of the prologue to the rule reveal the importance of obedience in this way of life:

> Listen carefully, my son, to the master's instructions, and attend to them with the ear of your heart. This is advice from a father who loves you; welcome it, and faithfully put it into practice. The labor of obedience will bring you back to him from whom you had drifted through the sloth of disobedience ... This message of mine is for you, then, if you are ready to give up your own will, once and for all, and armed with the strong and noble weapons of obedience to do battle for the true King, Christ the Lord.[13]

Listen carefully, the first words addressed to the monk, evoking the original Latin sense of obedience. *Listen,* not only to the commands of one's superior, but *incline the ear of your heart.* Prepare yourself to hear when God may speak a divine word of life to you through your superiors or in the course of your everyday activities, offering you the way to return home to the One you seek but have lost due to disobedience. The way of return to God in cenobitic monasticism is the way of obedience to Christ through obedience to the Scriptures, the rule, and community superiors.

The practice of monastic obedience is part and parcel of Benedict's program of growth in humility, in twelve steps. The very first one underscores the importance of obedience in the monastic quest:

> The first step of humility is unhesitating obedience, which comes naturally to those who cherish Christ above all. Because of the holy service they have professed, or because of dread of hell and for the glory of everlasting life, they carry out the superior's order as promptly as if the command came from God himself ... This very obedience, however, will be acceptable to God and agreeable to men only if compliance with what is commanded is not cringing or sluggish or half-hearted, but free from any grumbling or any reaction of unwillingness ... If a disciple obeys grudgingly and grumbles, not only aloud but also in his heart, then, even though

---

13. RB preface..

he carries out the order, his action will not be accepted with favor by God, who sees that he is grumbling in his heart.[14]

The Benedictine rule of communal monastic life gradually became the primary expression of monasticism in western Christianity, reaching its greatest influence by the twelfth century. Community obedience to the rule was also the way of what was called "mutual obedience" among the members, offering them the way to share and perfect the love of Christ with one another.

The High- and Late-Medieval Periods

Between the eleventh and thirteenth centuries, the primarily rural structure of European society was challenged by a series of social developments related to the emergence and growth of city centers. The changes brought by the cities' new focus on a mercantile economy and its monetary remuneration, an increase of population mobility away from rural social structures that had been the principal guides of social relations and authority, and the appearance of city-based university centers, were some of the factors that led to theological and philosophical questions concerning authority, obedience, and, more foundationally, the question of basic equality among individuals regardless of social class.[15] While only the beginning of a process that would still require many centuries to be realized, questions of basic equality among individuals revived the early Christian ideal of equitable relationship among all of God's people in the theological synthesis of Scholasticism.

The thought of Thomas Aquinas shows a more theological understanding of obedience in relationship to the salvific obedience of Christ. It also explains that Jesus' passion and crucifixion did not occur as an obedient act toward a divine command that demanded his death, but rather as a self-giving act that was ultimately determined by his love of the Father.[16] Following the hierarchical understanding of the world and society of his time, Aquinas explains how an act of obedience would find special favor with God:

---

14. RB 5.
15. Porter, "Natural Equality," 277–79.
16. *Summa* III q. 47, art. 2, ads. 2, 3; art. 3, ad. 1.

> Among the moral virtues, the greater the thing which a man contemns that he may adhere to God, the greater the virtue. Now there are three kinds of human goods that man may contemn for God's sake. The lowest of these are external goods, the goods of the body take the middle place, and the highest are the goods of the soul; and among these the chief, in a way, is the will, in so far as, by his will, man makes use of all other goods. Therefore, properly speaking, the virtue of obedience, whereby we contemn our own will for God's sake, is more praiseworthy than the other moral virtues, which contemn other goods for the sake of God ... Hence Gregory [the Great] says (*Moral.* xxxv) that *obedience is rightly preferred to sacrifices, because by sacrifices another's body is slain whereas by obedience we slay our own will.*[17]

This emphasis on the human will as primary among the "goods of the soul" and sacrificed through obedience will figure heavily in most subsequent theological treatments of the spiritual life and in understanding one's foregoing of self-volition as the highest possible expression of love for God.

Obedience in the Modern Era

Reformation and Roman Catholic Reform

The early sixteenth-century Catholic Church was beset by many evils. Moral laxity was rife among many bishops and clergy. Pastoral care in many dioceses was poor due in part to many bishops who were mostly absent from their official sees. Once-venerable religious orders had lost much of their vigor, often due to the imposition of lay superiors who had scant connection with the demands of consecrated life. Martin Luther had produced his ninety-five theses in 1517 calling for church reform, and ecclesiastical authority was losing its influence amid growing dissent throughout Europe. While there were efforts among a few organized Christian groups to enkindle internal reform within the Roman church, they proved insufficient in themselves to reverse the decline.

The Council of Trent (1545–63) was a long-overdue response to the need for clarification and renewal in the areas of doctrine, internal order, and the place of the church in a threatening world, with referrals to the need for renewed and stricter religious obedience. The council ushered in the beginning of the Catholic Counter-Reformation, emphasizing obedience

---

17. *Summa* II-II, q. 104, art. 3, ad.

Christian Obedience to the Authority of Christ

to church authority as it proceeded to impose more limiting restrictions in many spheres of church concerns including liturgical practice, doctrine, and the life of clergy and consecrated religious. Pope Pius IV (1499–1565), the last pope to preside over the council, ratified its decrees in the bull *Benedictus Deus*. Affirming the council teachings, the pope called for obedience to them in stark terms:

> We do, by the tenor of this letter, confirm them, and ordain that they be received and observed. Moreover, in virtue of holy obedience, and under the penalties appointed by the sacred canons, and others more grievous, even those of deprivation, to be inflicted at our discretion, We do also command all and each of our venerable brethren, the patriarchs, archbishops, bishops, and all other prelates . . . that they cause the same to be inviolably observed, each by his own subjects, in so far as in any way concerns them; silencing gainsayers and the contumacious, by means of the sentences, censures, and ecclesiastical penalties also contained in the said decrees; even calling in, if need be, the help of the secular arm.[18]

In line with this attitude, a more ominous arm of Roman authority emerged in the church office of the inquisition that was represented among the Catholic kingdoms of Europe. A new and more vigorous demand of obedience to Roman ecclesiastical authority had emerged in response to the challenges of a changing world; the resulting ominous and stifling atmosphere, while imposed for the survival of the Catholic faith at a dangerous moment, would continue to be felt throughout church life over the following centuries.

The expressed need for reform and renewal of obedience to church authority was one significant influence upon the spirituality of Ignatius of Loyola as he formed the Society of Jesus. Ignatian Jesuit spirituality, with its accent on following God's will through prompt obedience to superiors, had a widespread influence on the active lifestyles and ministries of most religious congregations that appeared over the following centuries. An example of the Jesuit notion of obedience comes from Ignatius's hallmark 1553 "Letter on Obedience" to the Portuguese Jesuits, recalling them to honor the vow of obedience they had taken.

In the letter, Ignatius underscores three increasingly demanding ways in which a subject could obey a Jesuit superior. The first is simply to accept that the superior's order was to be accepted as the will of God for the subject.

---

18. Pius IV, *Benedictus Deus*, 271.

The second is, rather than complaining about the superior's decision, to inwardly propose to oneself the superior's possible reasons for the order and to accept them. The third attitude, especially problematic for contemporary readers, is the way of blind obedience—to carry out the superior's order without considering either the cost or even any apparent impossibility of doing so. Anticipating that some superiors might be tempted to abuse this latter way, Ignatius quickly adds that one should respond in blind obedience in cases where the action is not obviously sinful or would obviously run contrary to God's will.[19]

Other post-Tridentine Catholic spiritual writers addressed the renewed emphasis on the virtue of obedience for Catholic Christians who were serious about following the example of Jesus. In his *Introduction to the Devout Life,* Francis de Sales dedicated a chapter to the merits of practicing the virtue. Along with the virtues of chastity and poverty, and within the parameters of one's life direction, de Sales regarded obedience as an essential practice for those who desired to advance in the spiritual life.

De Sales noted that each person is presented with two classifications of obedience to consider. The first are "necessary" or obligatory instances of obedience, reflecting the social structure of his day, each offering a corresponding fuller or lesser fulfillment of the virtue.

> By reason of that which is of necessity, you must humbly obey your ecclesiastical superiors, such as the pope, your bishop, your parish priest, and those who have been commissioned by them. You must obey your civil superiors, such as your prince and the magistrates he has appointed for your well being; and you must obey your domestic superiors, your father and mother, your master and mistress. Such obedience is called necessary because none of us can exempt himself from the duty of obeying superiors to whom God has given authority to command and govern us, each in the department assigned to him. Hence you must of necessity obey their commands. To be perfect, you must follow their counsels as well, even their desires and inclinations, as far as charity and prudence will permit. Obey them when they order something you like, for instance, to eat or take recreation. Although it seems no great virtue to obey in such cases, it would be very wrong to disobey . . . Obey in matters that are disagreeable, severe, and difficult, and that will be perfect obedience. In short, obey meekly and without arguing, quickly and without delay, cheerfully and without complaining. Above all, obey

---

19. Letter of March 26, 1553 to the members of the society in Portugal. Ignatius of Loyola, *Letters,* 287–95.

lovingly out of love of him who for love of us "made himself obedient unto death, even death on a cross," and as St. Bernard says, chose to lose life rather than obedience.[20]

The second category or "voluntary" invitations to obedience, according to de Sales, are worth more in God's eyes precisely because of their nonobligatory nature:

> We term obedience voluntary when we obligate ourselves by our own choice and when this choice is not imposed on us by someone else. Ordinarily a man does not choose his own prince, bishop, father, or mother and often women do not choose their husbands. However, each one chooses his own confessor and director. It may be that in making this choice we also make a vow to obey him . . . or without making a vow we dedicate ourselves to obey someone. Such obedience is called voluntary since it results from our own free will and choice.[21]

Noteworthy among this latter group was de Sales's view that God's will could be manifest to a Christian through obediently following the suggestions of a confessor or other director of their spiritual life. This spiritual guidance could also take the form of a personal program or rule of daily prayers and devotional practices that was approved by one's spiritual director, effectively bearing the force of God's will for the directee.[22] De Sales offered a decidedly positive and plausible vision of following a path of obedience for persons who strove to read God's perceived direction for them.

Another influential and more demanding attitude toward obedience is found in the thought of Jean-Jacques Olier. The academic and spiritual formation of clergy was a pressing concern of the reforming Council of Trent and Olier sought to further the reform efforts of the Catholic Church in France; towards this end, he established in 1642 the seminary of Saint-Sulpice. Following the belief of the time that exercising the virtue of obedience was the antidote *par excellence* to the chaos wrought by the original disobedience of Adam and Eve and borne by their descendants, Olier strove to instill in his seminarians a love for the virtue in imitation of

---

20. de Sales, *Introduction* 3.11.
21. de Sales, *Introduction* 3.11.
22. The practice of following a spiritual rule of life finds its roots in the early centuries of monastic life. From later medieval times into today, following a personal rule of life has been popular among Christians of all vocations who are intent to follow a more structured and focused interior life in the face of cultural indifference and adversity.

Jesus. Nineteenth-century biographer Edward Healey Thompson described Olier's zeal for this:

> Thus obedience was one of the virtues on which [Olier] laid the greatest stress. "Obedience," he was wont to say, "is the life of the children of the Church, the compendium of all virtues, the assured way to Heaven, an unfailing means for ascertaining the will of God, a fortress into which the devil has no access, one of the severest, but at the same time one of the sweetest, of martyrdoms, seeing that it makes us perfectly conformable to Jesus Christ. He who faithfully obeys the rule is invulnerable; whereas he who lets himself follow his own caprices lays himself open to the assaults of the enemy, and runs great risk of falling."[23]

Following Olier's guidance, daily seminary life was strictly regulated in keeping with the mandates of Trent and called for a seminarian's exacting obedience to priest-superiors. Thompson wrote that "no inmate of the house was to step outside the door, or pay or receive visits, without leave obtained of the Superior; and the observance of silence was so strictly enforced . . . that, except in time of recreation, not a word was spoken, although the Community consisted of more than a hundred persons."[24] Olier also stressed the value of obediently following a personal spiritual rule of life, especially among his seminarians, underscoring his serious concern for priestly reform in the wake of the Trent council:

> Fidelity to a rule formed the subject of the last capital lesson which M. Olier gave the young ecclesiastics on their quitting the Seminary to enter on their duties in the world. "If you observe a good rule of life, faithfully and out of love for the Lord," he would say to them, "you have everything to hope; you will live for God. But if you have no rule, or if you are not faithful in observing it, simply from motives of faith, as far as circumstances permit, you have everything to fear for your salvation; you are not living for God."[25]

The Post-Enlightenment Period

The changes in Western society that followed the onset of the seventeenth-century Enlightenment period brought both exhilaration and suffering. It

---

23. Thompson, *Life of Jean-Jacques Olier*, 450.
24. Thompson, *Life of Jean-Jacques Olier*, 450.
25. Thompson, *Life of Jean-Jacques Olier*, 450.

accelerated the gain of knowledge in the sciences and a deeper awareness and understanding of the human person. At the same time, its idealization of human reason, while desirable at one level, also hastened the decline of long-held traditional understandings of ecclesiastical and royal authority, of "cross and crown." The 1789 outbreak of the French Revolution inflamed the desire for a more autonomous rule and a classless society that quickly spread and whose agitations extended into the next century, leaving in its wake a path of bloodshed through much of Europe.[26]

This new outlook challenged the Catholic understanding of the world and society that had been systematized in its theology. For more than a century afterward, the Roman church would continue to assert itself as the authoritative channel of Christian revelation and salvation while insisting on obedience to church ecclesiastical structures, to a world that was growing indifferent to her claims. In the meantime, the twentieth century was to witness a new array of challenges in understanding Christian obedience to civil and religious authority.

II. TOWARDS A CONTEMPORARY APPRECIATION FOR CHRISTIAN OBEDIENCE

Twentieth-Century Challenges to Understanding Obedience and Authority

At its foundation, the practice of Christian obedience seeks to replicate Jesus' response to the love of his heavenly Father for the sake of reproducing his self-giving love to all other people, seeking to deepen one's relationship with God that Jesus exemplified in his faith-filled life and death. Western society has devalued this foundational understanding due to a contemporary skepticism toward obedience that would jeopardize personal freedom and is wary of both state and religious authority structures.

Apart from the authority exercised by ecclesiastical superiors, the Christian tradition has consistently viewed some form of civil authority as necessary to preserve order in societies that must contend with the reality of human weakness and sin. Secular rule participates or shares indirectly in the divine authority that is the source of all subservient ones; as such, civil authority merits the obedient submission of Christians, except in cases

---

26. See Jedin and Dolan, *History of the Church*, 6:342.

where civil authority demands one's compliance in some act that would be contrary to the gospel.

The existence in Western society of the "two swords" of spiritual and temporal authority from the later patristic through the early modern era often proved to be problematic, with their respective ends intertwining throughout the history of Christianity until recent centuries. The present-day regard for civil authority that considers itself no longer beholden to any religious influence has been largely a consequence of the upheaval wrought through the eighteenth-century Enlightenment period and the subsequent rise of secular civil governments.

The nineteenth-century developments that swept across Europe and indeed much of the world continued to have an effect into the twentieth, and with them came appalling wartime excesses of obedience and authority. Millions of Jews, ethnic itinerants, and countless others deemed as undesirable or social burdens were systematically exterminated in Nazi extermination camps before and during World War II. Many soldiers and other officials along the chain of command who bore responsibility defended themselves with the familiar claim that "I was only following orders." Not surprisingly, such horrific examples of misguided obedience would move any sane person to question the value of total obedience toward any authority system.

The revolutionary strains and unrest of the 1960s came to the United States along with a simmering skepticism toward traditional authority structures of government and religion. Major events such as protests against the American military involvement and resulting loss of life in southeast Asia, and the 1972 Watergate burglary and cover-up that toppled the Nixon presidency, left a collective scar on the psyche of a generation of Americans that resulted in considerable mistrust and skepticism toward civil authority. In the religious sphere, the more recent sex-abuse scandal within the Roman Catholic Church and the attempts of some bishops to minimize its impact "for the good of the church" have deeply affected its mission of proclaiming the Christian gospel and moral wisdom to an already-skeptical society.

Some Who Courageously Followed Christian Obedience in Jesus' Footsteps

Within the Christian churches, there have been notable dedicated individuals who struggled to live their faith in the world with a sense of

Christian Obedience to the Authority of Christ

obedience to the gospel message of Jesus while also respecting legitimate authority structures; only a handful can be mentioned here who have managed to walk along this narrow way. Among Roman Catholics, Dorothy Day (1897–1980) brought to her newfound Christian life a thirst for living the gospel of social justice; this onetime political anarchist routinely followed the way of Christ and the gospel by way of nonviolent civil protest for peace and the marginalized of society. A contemporary of Day, Thomas Merton (1915–68) also strove to live his monastic vow of obedience in a way that was both respectful of legitimate church and monastic authority while also expressing his deep conviction to peace, writing against war and the nuclear arms race.[27]

Other twentieth-century Christians have suffered violence and death while striving to remain obedient to the gospel when it conflicted with secular truths. Members of Germany's Evangelical "Confessing Church" persistently spoke out against the evils of National Socialism; several, including the theologian and pastor Dietrich Bonhoeffer (1906–45), paid with their lives for their faithfulness to the Christian message. In the United States, the Rev. Martin Luther King Jr. (1929–68) inspired many Americans of all races to confront racial prejudice in law and society through the way of gospel-inspired nonviolence and community witness, leading to his assassination. Other martyred Christian figures include Archbishop Oscar Romero (in 1980) and four Maryknoll-sponsored women in El Salvador (in the same year),[28] all of whom gave their lives for their defiance of government injustice on behalf of the suffering poor around them. In Brazil, Sister Dorothy Stang, SND (1931–2005) was shot for her efforts to defend the gift of the rain forest that is meant for all people, rather than to be exploited by a powerful few. The life and death of these individuals gave witness to obeying the gospel message as their highest priority, even when it brought them into violent conflict with civil law and ideologies.

---

27. To read more on Merton's struggle to observe Christian obedience as a monk in his demanding time, see the article by Ciraulo, "Thomas Merton's Creative (dis)Obedience," 189–219.

28. The names of these four women were Maura Clark, Jean Donovan, Ita Ford, and Dorothy Kazel.

From Strength to Strength

Identifying One's Individual Path of Christian Obedience

While most Christians will not be called to walk the way of physical martyrdom for their fidelity to the gospel, the challenge to live more deliberately the virtue of Christian obedience in daily life still beckons many disciples to a deeper assimilation of Jesus' life example. Following the way of Christian obedience requires the willingness and ability to listen intently for the divine voice calling us to gospel-inspired lives in everyday moments.

A life of Christian obedience, while not always easy to observe, is usually not difficult to determine. For most people, their particular adult calling or path in life defines the parameters that help to frame their way of Christian obedience. In addition to loving God and others according to the example of Jesus that all disciples are called to follow, married spouses are continually challenged to live in a way that helps the other to find Christ who is present in their relationship. Parents are called to attend to the needs of their children. Those appointed to ministry and leadership have the call to follow the example of the faithful, self-giving Christ in the midst of their flock. Those who live together as consecrated members of religious congregations typically follow a more defined program of vowed obedience, seeking to reproduce the presence of Christ among themselves and beyond through mutual self-giving and communal harmony. Each of these life paths will provide everyday moments in which to respond to the Father's love for us by our loving one another through following the example of Jesus.

Within each life, however, there will be times when following the way of Jesus is not so simple. It can be costly to one's personal reputation, or perhaps even bring some degree of physical violence toward oneself or one's family. Employees who observe an unjust practice in the workplace must decide whether they should speak out as Christ and risk losing their employment. Those who seek to be faithful Christian citizens may be moved to either support or oppose a law that is discriminatory toward a particular ethnic or racial group. One vowed to consecrated religious life may be directed by a superior in a way that appears to run contrary to basic Christian respect for one's human dignity or personal talents. Following Christian obedience sometimes may call one to stand and speak against what is a patently sinful practice; at other times it will require listening more intently to determine the better choice between two good options through the practice of Christian spiritual discernment.[29]

---

29. Spiritual discernment involves a process leading to making a choice between two

Christian Obedience in Relationships with God, with Others, and as Part of Creation

Having surveyed the historical progression of understanding and living the virtue of Christian obedience through the present day, we are now in a position to suggest an integral view of practicing the virtue. How is Christian obedience rooted in our relationship with God in Christ? How does it proceed to affect other people in the world? How can exercising the virtue lead us to a more integral existence as part of the created world?

With God

At its root, a disciple practicing Christian obedience seeks to follow Jesus' attitude of self-giving love toward his Father as the all-encompassing fulfillment of the Jewish covenant relationship with God. The fulfillment of the covenant law was the Jewish response in faith to the God who chose to make of them a great nation, a people set apart. The totally other-centered love of Jesus for his Father and for those whom his Father loved forms the paradigm for fulfilling that law perfectly, beyond any written code. As his disciples, on our way to becoming transformed into Christ, we seek to make present in our world and time his life of deepest love that fulfilled the law. Obedience for the Christian is to regard all of life and all people in the manner that Jesus did, thereby hearing and responding to the Fathers command that "here is my beloved Son, listen to him" (Mark 9:7).

With Others

My practice of Christian obedience, following the example of Jesus in my relationship with both God and others, can lead me to experience a growing harmony with the Spirit that empowers my discipleship. This attitude does two things. It will slowly bring about an abiding interior joy as my life increasingly harmonizes with the divine plan for me; also, my lived witness of growing closeness to God through Christ has the potential to proclaim

---

good options, made in faith and the belief that one option is closer to the particular path that God truly intends for the person in light of that person's responsibilities to family, community, and Christian community. The practice of Christian discernment has existed from the earliest Christian centuries; one popular way is known through the fifteenth-century *Spiritual Exercises* of Ignatius of Loyola. More recent books on present-day spiritual discernment include that of Elizabeth Liebert, *Way of Discernment*.

to others the presence of Christ through my lived faith-witness to others around me. For some, this fidelity will be costly in terms of physical suffering, persecution, and even martyrdom as their perception of God's plan brings them into conflict with the value systems of others. The difficulty is that my deepest inner peace will result only to the extent of harmonizing my life with the divine inner prompting within me, resulting in an unshakeable inner sense of integrity through following the deep inspiration of the Holy Spirit. Far more often, though, my practice of Christian obedience through extending the love of Christ will be exercised in the more mundane acts of self-giving love that present themselves during the day, the occasions of everyday obedience along the "little way" that was popularized by the nineteenth-century Carmelite Thérèse of Lisieux.

As Part of Creation

The created world is subject to certain spiritual and physical laws that are essential to its existence. Our imitation of Christ follows the divine law meant for humanity to observe, so to live a fully human life as sons and daughters of God and to find, if you will, the original "inner balance" that God intended for us. The entirety of creation of which we are part is likewise subject to another set of natural laws, determined by the divine source of all that exists, supporting the intricate series of harmonious relationships on which the earthly creation depends for its existence. At the cosmic level, the centripetal force of gravity finds its equilibrium against the opposing centrifugal force of outward movement, combining to hold the earth in a delicate life-sustaining orbit around the sun. On the earth's surface, the alternating cycles of day and night, of sunshine and rain, have their effect on whatever vegetation that lives in a particular geographical area as well as their eventual regeneration of the soil through decomposition. Everywhere on earth, one will find geographically-sensitive ecosystems with a particular balance of nature that is necessary for the survival and thriving of its plants, its animal life, and our mutual coexistence. Should a particular ecosystem lose its delicate balance for some reason, the resulting effect can have devastating consequences at the local, regional, and even worldwide levels.

The reorientation of one's free will to the practice of Christian obedience, following the example of Jesus' historical life in his relationship with other persons, carries with it a desire for the original interpersonal harmony that is meant to be ours. By extension, a human life that more conscientiously respects and lives according to the divinely-inspired balance of creation will contribute to the overall interspecies balance and interrelationship contained in creation. The papal encyclical *Laudato Si'* expresses this by stating that all of creation is interrelated as a result of our common created state that has emerged from our creator, likewise existing as a harmonious interrelationship of one God in a Trinity of divine Persons:

> The divine Persons are subsistent relations, and the world, created according to the divine model, is a web of relationships. Creatures tend towards God, and in turn it is proper to every living being to tend towards other things, so that throughout the universe we can find any number of constant and secretly interwoven relationships. This leads us not only to marvel at the manifold connections existing among creatures, but also to discover a key to our own fulfilment. The human person grows more, matures more and is sanctified more to the extent that he or she enters into relationships, going out from themselves to live in communion with God, with others and with all creatures. In this way, they make their own that trinitarian dynamism which God imprinted in them when they were created. Everything is interconnected, and this invites us to develop a spirituality of that global solidarity which flows from the mystery of the Trinity.[30]

"Everything is interconnected..." To the degree that I live in harmony with the divine law of God in Christ that has been written in my heart, and let that direct my relationships with other people around me and throughout the world, I will grow to respect others' legitimate right to the goods and gifts of creation that we all share and with which we are interrelated as cocreated beings. My Christian discipleship, when lived in obedience to the life example of Jesus in his way of relating to his Father and in respecting the humanity of others, thus participates in the divine task of restoring the initial harmony of all creation as it should exist in the reign of God, subject to the authority of God in Christ Jesus.

---

30. Francis, *Laudato Si'*, no. 240.

4

Chastity Leading to Deeper Christian Love

HUMAN SEXUALITY IS A powerful force. Ronald Rolheiser in *The Holy Longing* refers to it as divine fire. A divinely-sourced creative energy, human sexuality has the potential to carry one to the summit of human bliss, or to wreak emotional destruction lasting for one's lifetime; it can also be channeled in the service of ever-deepening love, or allowed to spread like wildfire capable of destroying lives, families, and even society.

The Christian virtue of chastity keeps guard over the senses and seeks to regulate the expression of our natural sexual appetite, depending on one's marital state in life. Conjugal chastity honors rightly ordered conjugal sexual love between a married man and woman while proscribing any sexual activity outside the relationship. Those Christians who are unmarried are called to observe continent chastity, abstaining from all physical sexual expression proper to marriage. Celibate chastity aids individuals who, following a vow or similar promise, are committed to abstinence from all sexual activity and exclude the possibility of marriage (the usual route for Roman Catholic clergy, for example). Consecrated or vowed chastity is the way of both men and women who embrace consecrated religious life, committing them to observe interior and exterior sexual purity (the avoidance of sexually erotic or "lustful" thoughts or behavior) in order to follow more fully the way of Jesus in the reign of God. The Christian virtue of chastity, in effect, regulates a Christian disciple's statement of interior and exterior sexual integrity according to his or her relationship with a Christian married spouse and other acquaintances.

Each of these ways of living the Christian virtue of chastity has its roots in early Christianity, each having developed at its own pace while influenced by attitudes toward the others, offering different ways of living Christian discipleship as a sexual being. How Christians regarded the virtue of chastity at any historical moment has been directly affected by how they appreciated the place and practice of human sexuality and its "proper" and "improper" exercise. The Christian tradition concerning sex has evolved throughout its history into the present day, revealing changes in the moral understanding and acceptance of sexual intercourse, marriage, and the practice of sexual continence in lifelong celibacy and Christian virginity.

I. CHRISTIAN CHASTITY THROUGH THE CENTURIES

What would eventually become the Judeo-Christian regard for chastity and continence was influenced, at different moments, by the surrounding Greek and Roman empires. Both were patriarchal, in which women had limited individual rights. Both culture held a more cavalier and utilitarian attitude toward human sexual activity in whatever form, corresponding with the ways that they were attentive to the natural fecundity of the earth and livestock. Since love was not usually an initial concern in marriage, primarily meant to produce legitimate heirs (hopefully male), it was socially acceptable for a husband to have an extramarital paramour; wives, however, could not, at least not without great discretion. Temple prostitution was an acceptable practice, as well as sexual encounters between same-sex partners, whether adult-adult or adult-child. The early Christian call for monogamous and faithful marriage that shunned extramarital sexual activity would have sounded alien in the midst of such a background.

Greek Neo-Platonist and Stoic philosophies, with their preference for the world of ideas over the created material world of human caprice and imperfection and the triumph of the soul over the body and its various swirling passions, helped to shape early Christian exaltation of virginity and celibacy over marriage. Also, Stoicism supported the idea that activities of intellect and contemplation, traditionally seen as male pursuits, suffered as a result of one's pursuits in the material world, including marriage, family, and sexual intercourse (for which procreation was the only worthy justification). As Judeo-Christianity eventually absorbed some Platonist and Stoic influences of Greek culture through the steady influx of Greek-speaking and Hellenist-Jewish converts, early Christian influential writers shared the popular belief that while sex within marriage was an acceptable good, at least periodic continence was better, and lifelong virginity was the best and most desirable way for Christian living.

Chastity in Scripture

The Old Testament

Primitive Christianity's regard for marriage and continence was initially affected by the Hebrew tradition in which it was rooted. Celibacy and continence by and large did not have a place in the Jewish culture that had received the divine mandate to produce offspring, to "be fruitful and multiply" (Gen 1:28), apart from some prophetic or ascetical movements such as the Essenes and the *Therapeutae*.[1] As in the Greek and Roman worlds, ancient Hebrew tradition also bore a great disparity of regard for men and women, notably concerning marriage and sexual mores.[2] There is no specific mention in the Old Testament of chastity as a virtue, though we do find some instruction to curb one's sexual activity, most notably in cases of adulterous relationships. The taking of the married spouse of another, proscribed by the of the sixth and ninth commandments of the Decalogue, was a serious infraction warranting divine retribution. For example, King David's desire for Uriah's husband Bathsheba resulted in the murder of her husband; even before the illicit birth of Absalom, the prophet Nathan informed the king that, although God forgave David's grievous behavior, his injustice would result in the tragic death of his son.[3]

---

1. Members of an ancient monastic community of Egyptian Jewish ascetics.

2. Under Hebraic law, men fared differently than women concerning the areas of sexual behavior and relations. The patriarchal culture meant that men were given first consideration in forming new family alliances. Socially, a woman was regarded as somewhere between a person and a possession, first under the care of her father and family who would eventually entrust her in marriage to a husband (Exod 20–21). Sexually-inclined visitors to Lot's house wanted to "know" his two male guests; to protect them, Lot gave up one of his two daughters (Gen 19:4–8). Women who entered into marriage could be stoned if she was found not to be a virgin (Deut 22:13–21). A woman who was sexually violated within the city walls could be stoned if it was determined that she did not cry out aloud to be heard during the assault; this penalty was relaxed if the attack occurred away from people in the countryside (Deut 22:23–27).

3. 2 Sam 11:1—12:25.

Chastity Leading to Deeper Christian Love

Among the wisdom literature, the fifth chapter of Proverbs advises a young man to refrain from sexual activity with harlots, notably temple prostitutes of the surrounding Canaanite culture. True happiness for the youth would rather be found in the embrace of his lawful wife; dalliances with "loose women" (verse 3) would only prove disastrous:

> Keep your way far from her, and do not go near the door of her house; or you will give your honor to others, and your years to the merciless, and strangers will take their fill of your wealth, and your labors will go to the house of an alien; and at the end of your life you will groan, when your flesh and body are consumed, and you say, "Oh, how I hated discipline and my heart despised reproof! I did not listen to the voice of my teachers or incline my ear to my instructors."[4]

Physical sexual relations with a woman married to another man was an egregious sin, proscribed in the Decalogue and denounced by the wisdom teacher. Such activity could only rupture the deeply-revered Hebrew bond of the marriage covenant and family life; indeed, the teacher reminds the son that one who sows discord in a family commits an offense especially detested by the Lord (Prov 6:16–19). Committing adultery would surely do such and incur the husband's wrath:

> Do not desire her beauty in your heart, and do not let her capture you with her eyelashes; for a prostitute's fee is only a loaf of bread, but the wife of another stalks a man's very life. Can fire be carried in the bosom without burning one's clothes? Or can one walk on hot coals without scorching the feet? So is he who sleeps with his neighbor's wife; no one who touches her will go unpunished . . . For jealousy arouses a husband's fury, and he shows no restraint when he takes revenge.[5]

Concerning the pursuit of sexual restraint, it is worth noting that sexual self-regulation in these cases required the cultivation of personal discipline and the desire for wisdom, ideally instilled by one's parents from a young age, forming the foundation to seek wisdom through life as one's greatest prize.[6]

---

4. Prov 5:8–13.
5. Prov 6:25–29; 34.
6. Bilezikian, "Discipline," 631–32.

From Strength to Strength

The New Testament

The time of both Jesus and the apostle Paul was steeped in the Hebrew spiritual tradition in which one's body, soul, spirit, were all understood in an interrelated unity that was animated by the degree of one's purity or "singleness of heart." For the Jews, the heart represented one's spiritual center, replete with inner motivations and inclinations to both evil and good. Theirs was a lifelong struggle to follow good inclinations of the heart in order to live justly, mercifully, and at peace with all persons, neighbor and stranger alike, following the Jewish laws and traditions that promoted family, offspring, and a growing nation. The appearance of Jesus and his disciples as a band of continent men would have recalled to the Hebrew mind the practiced celibacy in its prophetic tradition and eschatological movements. For the wider Jewish community, however, such movements of vagabond spirit-driven celibates could be regarded as threatening to the cherished Jewish desire for family and social order and held little social value for them.

Jesus of the synoptic Gospels, while traditionally understood to have followed celibate continence during his ministerial life, neither demanded continence from his followers nor did he expressly present his solitary lifestyle as being superior to marriage. In Matthew 19:12, he proclaimed that some individuals are indeed moved to renounce marriage, effectively becoming eunuchs because of their all-consuming quest to welcome the emerging Reign of God. The Matthean Jesus speaks the word *eunuch* several times in these verses, leading some commentators to speculate that Jesus was purposely using a word that for the Jews was derisive and likely used against him and his followers.[7] Elsewhere in Matthew, Jesus gives his teaching on divorce through reinforcing the permanency and sacred quality of marriage.[8]

Contrary to the limited Gospel evidence for concern over sexual ethics, the apostle Paul was considerably more taken with the issue. Paul taught among his recent Gentile-Christian converts that one must learn to live following Christian sexual integrity in the midst of their surrounding pagan culture that held a more relaxed view toward such practices as prostitution, homosexuality, and pederasty. Apparently, at least some of Paul's converts from elsewhere had left behind some of these practices (1

---

7. Quinn, "Continence," 43.
8. Matt 19:3–9; see also Mark 10:2–12; Luke 16:18.

Cor 6:9–11); it would be understandable that breaking away from older habits and lifestyles takes time and determination, especially while temptations surrounded them. Self-control was essential to their quest to achieve singleness of heart as Christian disciples; Paul reminded the Thessalonian Christians of this critical need, whether as abstinent single Christians or for those who embraced marriage:

> For this is the will of God, your sanctification; that you abstain from fornication [*porneia*]; that each one of you know how to control your own body [*skenos*, "vessel"] in holiness and honor, not with lustful passion, like the Gentiles who do not know God, that no one wrong or exploit a brother or sister in this matter . . . For God did not call us to impurity but in holiness. Therefore whoever rejects this rejects not human authority but God, who also gives his Holy Spirit to you.[9]

Despite some popular misconception, Paul respected the sanctifying capacity of marriage.[10] He also noted that married life could lead to holiness since it offered a legitimate, holy, and fruitful way to channel the overpowering human sexual desire, considered a formidable obstacle to realizing single-heartedness (1 Cor 7:1–4). Before dismissing this as some overzealous religious statement, though, one should first consider the context for Paul's teaching in light of his evangelical mission.

Paul and the first Christians believed that Jesus' return was immanent, no doubt before the end of their lifetimes, and that they should prepare themselves. He taught that a disciple's singleness of heart was of primary importance to be ready for the Lord at the moment of his return. The Corinthian church presented Paul with several moral questions that concerned them during their days and weeks and months of waiting. We find that some people wanted to follow Paul's celibate lifestyle, while others were drawn to marriage. Some widows wished to remarry; still others felt that perhaps they should leave their nonbelieving spouse to prepare more fully for Jesus' return. Paul's advice to them concerning marriage or celibacy was that *it is better for you to remain in the state that you were in when you first accepted the Lord*. The day draws short, he warned; the hour was near for Christ to return, so prepare for his coming by cultivating an undivided heart fixed on the Lord in whatever state of life in which you were called. Having said that, Paul also noted that it would be better for

---

9. 1 Thess 4:3–8.
10. 1 Cor 7:13–14; see also Eph 5:22–32.

those unmarried Christians to maintain their continent celibacy, as he did, so to give oneself more fully to serving the Lord and await the *parousia* with an undivided heart. Those who were married, while concerned to attend to the Lord, were also anxious to please their spouse, hence his wish that "all were as I myself am" (1 Cor 7:7). Paul also noted that temporary sexual continence for a married couple was an acceptable practice for the sake of fostering a more intense prayer life (7:3–5).

One other celibate group that we find mentioned in some of the New Testament writings is the beginning of a recognized association of widows who chose celibacy over remarriage. The New Testament Greek word for "widow" (*kheiras*) was not limited to those women who remained alone after their husbands had died but could include older women who for some reason no longer lived with their living spouse, or even those who had never married.[11] Paul mentions them in 1 Corinthians 7, as does the author of the first letter to Timothy. After reminding the local church of their responsibility to provide for the material needs of these women in the absence of capable family members, Timothy indicates the presence among them of a particular group with specific requirements:

> Let a widow be put on the list if she is not less than sixty years old and has been married only once; she must be well attested for her good works, as one who has brought up children, shown hospitality, washed the saints' feet, helped the afflicted, and devoted herself to doing good in every way . . . But refuse to put younger widows on the list; for when their sensual desires alienate them from Christ, they want to marry, and so they incur condemnation for having violated their first pledge.[12]

In summary, we find in the Scriptures that sexual continence, celibacy, and marriage were all respected observances. While being less attractive to the Jewish audience, Christian celibacy could aid disciples to more attentively await the return of the Lord; for married disciples, periodic (and mutually-accepted) continence was also acceptable in the interest of nurturing more intensive prayer. Widows and other single women could embrace a life of celibacy as members of a select group that offered both spiritual and corporeal assistance to the local Christian community. Observing continence was considered to be a more expeditious way to realize

---

11. Quinn, "Continence," 47.
12. 1 Tim 5:9–10; 11–12.

the singleness of heart that was at the center of the Jewish religion, and for Christians intent on preparing for Christ's return.

The Christian community honored marriage as a holy and permanent state, following Jesus' teaching and also upheld by Paul, though the latter saw one reason for marriage as a concession to the weakness of the flesh. Physical sexual expression outside marriage and the numerous possible sexual aberrations outside marriage (the various forms of *pornea*) were considered to be irreconcilable with Christian moral life.

Chastity in the Patristic Era

The Church Fathers

By the end of the second century, lifelong continence through committed virginity was a highly-praised attribute for disciples who would seriously pursue Christian discipleship. Besides their mention in some of the New Testament pastoral letters, we find Clement of Rome extolling the virgins of Corinth, while Ignatius of Antioch acknowledging those of Smyrna while on the way to martyrdom in Rome.[13] The Roman *Shepherd of Hermas*, in the ninth and tenth similitudes, portrays a group of virgins as having an important role in helping to build up the church, while Origen in his letter *Against Celsus* (7.48) complements those living in Alexandria. It is apparent that the practice of virginity was widespread and well-regarded throughout the Christian world.

The early church fathers widely recognized marriage as a worthy life for Christian disciples, though more as being a concession to an unruly sexual drive. One's pesky and unmanageable urges would be better confined to a stable marriage arrangement with a spouse, thereby lessening the possibility of falling prey to the more libertine sexual observances of the surrounding pagan society. Continence and especially the practice of virginity were considered better for the sake of focusing on prayer and the pursuit of wisdom, with most of the fathers expressing the opinion that married life burdened Christian disciples with concerns of the material world and other pursuits of the flesh. They generally held in common the thought of Justin Martyr (ca. 100–ca. 165) that intercourse in marriage was meant exclusively for the purpose of procreation and raising children; otherwise, married Christians

---

13. Ign. *Smyrn.* 13.

were expected to follow a rationally-guided life of sexual continence.[14] This attitude also affected a commonly-shared patristic attitude toward remarriage, that doing so was contrary to God having called one man to one woman in the first marriage. They also considered second marriages (more so in the case of a third!) as concessions for Christians who could not control their sexual desires, having absolutely no proper place in the lives of those dedicated to the clergy or committed widows.

The esteem for Christian virginity as an ascetical practice would only grow during the first Christian centuries. Those men or women practicing Christian celibacy served as reminders to the wider Christian community that they, too, were challenged to live as people firm in their faith in a perilous time. Early Christians lived with the frequent threat of persecution and martyrdom that could swoop down upon them at the whim of the emperor or even the local authority. Bishops would continually exhort their flocks to fortify themselves with the disciplines of prayer and detachment from earthly goods so that they might not falter during such moments. Those who practiced Christian virginity undertook a socially recognized ascetical struggle that presumed a disciplined life of prayer and the cultivation of Christian virtue in order to preserve it. They were in effect Christian athletes in the midst of their communities, reminding others of the universal challenge to seek Christ as their one true good, as an ancient writer noted:

> Those, therefore, who imitate Christ, imitate Him earnestly. For those who have "put on Christ" in truth, express His likeness in their thoughts, and in their whole life, and in all their behaviour: in word, and in deeds, and in patience, and in fortitude, and in knowledge, and in chastity, and in long-suffering, and in a pure heart, and in faith, and in hope, and in full and perfect love towards God . . . For every virgin who is in God is holy in her body and in her spirit, and is constant in the service of her Lord, not turning away from it any whither, but waiting upon Him always in purity and holiness in the Spirit of God, being "solicitous how she may please her Lord," by living purely and without stain, and solicitous to be pleasing before Him in every thing.[15]

The bishop Clement of Alexandria (150–217), another proponent of Christian virginity, also wrote in defense of marriage while facing incursions

---

14. Justin, *1 Apol.* 29.

15. Pseudo-Clement, (first) *Letter to Virgins* 7. Once attributed to Clement of Rome, it likely was written sometime in the early third century.

of Gnosticism that were finding their way into his church community. While praising the state of continence or virginity for those able to accept it,[16] Clement taught that marriage was something good rather than an evil consequence of the first sin, a state of life that contributed to the happiness of the couple so long as the partners were not driven by inordinate sexual desire.[17] Those who were married should rather be living in every way according to their will guided by reason; marital relations were for the sake of procreation and should be honored as such between husband and wife:

> In general, let our affirmation about marriage, food and the rest proceed: we should never act from desire; our will should be concentrated on necessities. We are children of will, not of desire. If a man marries in order to have children he ought to practice self-control. He ought not to have a sexual desire even for his wife, to whom he has a duty to show Christian love. He ought to produce children by a reverent, disciplined act of will. We have learned not "to pay attention to physical desires," "walking decorously as in the light of day"—that is, in Christ and the shining conduct of the Lord's way—"not in drunken carousing, sexual promiscuity, or jealous quarreling."[18]

Clement's writings bear some influences of Stoicism that placed an exalted value on one's personal development of *apathea* (literally, "passionlessness"), allowing procreation as the only acceptable reason for participating in marital relations rather than consenting to unbridled lust. Responding to such heated passion, for Clement, placed a married couple on the level of nonrational animals.[19]

Tertullian bears a reputation as a rigorist and extreme ascetic, especially following his years in the Montanist reform movement. Still, the theologian of Carthage recognized marriage in a holy light while placing a higher value on sexual abstinence, even if temporarily observed by a married couple for spiritual purposes:

> For we do not reject marriage, but simply refrain from it. Nor do we prescribe sanctity as the rule, but only recommend it, observing it as a good, yea, even the better state, if each man uses it carefully according to his ability; but at the same time earnestly vindicating

---

16. Clement of Alexandria, *Strom.* 3.50.
17. Clement of Alexandria, *Strom.* 2.139–40.
18. Clement of Alexandria, *Strom.* 3.58.
19. Clement of Alexandria, *Strom.* 3.67.

marriage, whenever hostile attacks are made against it as a polluted thing, to the disparagement of the Creator. For He bestowed His blessing on matrimony also, as on an honorable estate, for the increase of the human race; as He did indeed on the whole of His creation, for wholesome and good uses.[20]

Elsewhere, in a touching letter to his wife that likely was written before his Montanist days, Tertullian portrays a beautiful early picture of what marriage was meant to be for Christian couples:

> How beautiful, then, the marriage of two Christians, two who are one in hope, one in desire, one in the way of life they follow, one in the religion they practice. They are as brother and sister, both servants of the same Master. Nothing divides them, either in flesh or in spirit. They are, in very truth, two in one flesh; and where there is but one flesh there is also but one spirit. They pray together, they worship together, they fast together; instructing one another, encouraging one another, strengthening one another. Side by side they visit God's church and partake of God's Banquet; side by side they face difficulties and persecution, share their consolations. They have no secrets from one another; they never shun each other's company; they never bring sorrow to each other's hearts ... They need not be furtive about making the Sign of the Cross, nor timorous in greeting the brethren, nor silent in asking a blessing of God. Psalms and hymns they sing to one another, striving to see which one of them will chant more beautifully the praises of their Lord. Hearing and seeing this, Christ rejoices. To such as these He gives His peace. Where there are two together, there also He is present; and where He is, there evil is not.[21]

Tertullian's fellow Carthaginian, Cyprian, expressed with delight the glories of virginal chastity for both men and women, calling them "the flower of the ecclesiastical seed, the grace and ornament of spiritual endowment, a joyous disposition, the wholesome and uncorrupted work of praise and honour, God's image answering to the holiness of the Lord, the more illustrious portion of Christ's flock."[22] Cyprian exhorted his virginal audience to a lifestyle devoid of the entrapments of wealth, adornment,

---

20. Tertullian, *Marc.* 1.29.

21. Tertullian, *Ux.* 2.8. Guided by a principal shared by many of the early church fathers, Tertullian's underlying purpose for the letter was to exhort his wife to forego remarriage if he should die before her or, if she must remarry, then do so with another Christian.

22. Cyprian, *Hab. virg.* 3.

hair dressing, and social situations such as wedding celebrations and public baths that would severely test their lofty aspirations.

Cyprian likewise held positive regard for Christians who lived in the married state. A life of virginity expressed chastity's highest degree, followed by those observing continence, then among those who were married; nonetheless, chastity was gloriously found in each of the three according to one's particular marital state.[23] Indeed, marriage had its particular glory pointing to the love of Christ:

> For both her own husband belongs to the woman, for the reason that besides him she may know no other; and the woman is given to the man for the purpose that, when that which had been his own had been yielded to him, he should seek for nothing belonging to another. And in such wise it is said, "Two shall be in one flesh," that what had been made one should return together, that a separation without return should not afford any occasion to a stranger ... [*the apostle Paul*] says: "Because he who loves his wife, loves himself. For no one hates his own flesh; but nourishes and cherishes it, even as Christ the Church." From this passage there is great authority for charity with chastity, if wives are to be loved by their husbands even as Christ loved the Church and wives ought so to love their husbands also as the Church loves Christ.[24]

Cyprian, nonetheless, argued that virginity should be the preference of women, for reasons both spiritual and practical:

> [Virginity] places itself on an equality with angels; moreover, if we investigate, it even excels them, because struggling in the flesh it gains the victory even against a nature which angels have not. What else is virginity than the glorious preparation for the future life? Virginity is of neither sex. Virginity is the continuance of infancy. Virginity is the triumph over pleasures. Virginity has no children; but what is more, it has contempt for offspring: it has not fruitfulness, but neither has it bereavement; blessed that it is free from the pain of bringing forth; more blessed still that it is free from the calamity of the death of children. What else is virginity than the freedom of liberty? It has no husband for a master. Virginity is freed from all affections: it is not given up to marriage, nor

---

23. Cyprian, *Util. disc.* 4.
24. Cyprian, *Util. disc.* 5.

to the world, nor to children. It cannot dread persecution, since it cannot provoke it from its security.[25]

Chapters 2 and 3 of the *Teaching of the Apostles* (the *Didaschalia apostolorum*) also offer some faith-based practical advice for early third-century Christian convert husbands and wives in their desire to faithfully live their mutual calling. The person of Christ should be recognizable in the actions of each partner toward the other; the man in his loving mercy and forbearance toward his wife, and the wife's corresponding respect for Christ represented in the husband.

We find sufficient evidence, then, that the ante-Nicene Christian church fathers, despite their clear preference for those who observed virginity, were also concerned for the well-being and fidelity of those who chose marriage. Each way had its particular set of social and religious expectations in terms of sexual activity and public behavior.

Following the normalization of Christianity in the early fourth century and its rapid assimilation throughout the empire, the emergence of Christian monasticism marked the beginning of what we might call the institutionalization of Christian virginity. Fourth-century primitive monasticism records the flight of both men and women into the wilderness as solitaries who were guided by Scriptural reflection and accumulating wisdom, leading to the more organized cenobitic (community living) rules of Pachomias, Basil, Augustine of Hippo, and Benedict. Their ideal of material and sexual detachment for the sake of praising God through a life of prayer and obedience would bolster the understanding that true Christian discipleship required celibacy over marriage and the renunciation of worldly pursuits.

Developing the resources to live as chaste celibates was a significant topic for patristic writers such as John Chrysostom, Jerome (ca. 349–420), and Augustine of Hippo. Each one had pursued the monastic discipline in one form or another and could wax eloquently on committed virginity. Each also had his opinion on Christian marriage and could speak more or less positively about conjugal life and sexual activity, revealing some elements for what constituted Christian marital chastity.

Chrysostom emerged as the strongest defender of marriage and offered the most positive view of the married state. Contrary to the wider belief that procreation constituted the primary reason for marriage and engaging in sexual intercourse, he noted that there had to be more to

---

25. Cyprian, *Util. disc.* 7.

marriage since the ancient scriptural mandate in Genesis that was used to justify sexual relations, to "be fruitful and multiply," had long since been realized. Rather, in his words, the primary reason for marriage had become protecting the sexual integrity of the married couple, their faithfulness to each other:

> So there remains only one reason for marriage, to avoid fornication, and the remedy is offered for this purpose. If you are going to practice fornication after marriage, you have approached marriage uselessly and in vain; or rather not merely in vain, but to your harm.[26]

Chrysostom taught that both husband and wife had a shared responsibility to maintain the integrity of their relationship, following the oft-cited patristic phrase, originally Pauline, that "just as the husband is master of her body, so the wife is mistress of his body."[27] John still appealed to the traditional practice that the husband was to love his wife while she was to respect her husband. Here, though, John warned that the husband's task was the more demanding since, called to love his spouse in the same patient, forgiving, and unfailing way that Christ loves the church, his challenge to love a spouse was more difficult and all-consuming than her responsibility to respect one.[28]

Far from neglecting those who elected to follow the way of Christian virginity, Chrysostom encouraged the practice over marriage as the comparatively higher of the two states in life, seeing virgins as closer to the ranks of incorporeal angels who did not marry.[29]

The thought of Augustine of Hippo concerning marriage has influenced the Western church from the fifth century until the Second Vatican Council in the twentieth, and indeed may still be felt in the present day. As with many of the early church fathers, Augustine's initial thought on marriage and sexual relations were likely formed throughout his early life that included his years as a Manichaean, with its cavalier attitude toward sexual behavior and an abhorrence to procreation, after which he experienced the religious zeal of his early Christian years. His more mature experiences as bishop led him to defend the goodness of both marriage and virginity against those who saw no spiritual benefit to virginity over marriage (such

---

26. Chrysostom, "Sermon on Marriage," 86.
27. One place where this theme appears is in his sermon 20 on Eph 5:22–23.
28. Chrysostom, *Hom. Eph.* 5:22–33.
29. Chrysostom, *Virginit.* 11.1–2.

as the monk Jovinian) or who regarded marriage and marital sexual intercourse as evil (as found among the Manichaeans and Pelagians). Augustine also had to contend with an even more suppressive attitude toward marriage that had resulted from overly-zealous Christian defenders of virginity (such as Jerome).

In his work *On the Good of Marriage*, Augustine sets down that there are, in fact, three desirable and useful good reasons. The first is the procreation of children; next is the spouses' mutual fidelity to each other in marriage that restrains them from seeking to quench their powerful sexual desires through adultery and other extramarital sexual activity. The third benefit is that their union offers an indissoluble and visible "sacramental" (mysterious) sign of Christ's invisible and abiding union with the church. Although reasserting that celibate virginity is an objectively better state than marriage, the latter is nonetheless a meritorious Christian life that should instill respect and humility among those who follow the way of virginity.[30]

From the patristic era, we find that both marital and celibate forms of chastity underwent considerable development, in no small way influenced by the early Christian regard for sexual intercourse as acceptable solely for the cause of procreation (though not by all, as John Chrysostom claimed). Despite the persistent hierarchical view of "good versus better" that can be annoying to contemporary readers, there emerged a Christian vision for each way of life that would remain largely uncontested until the sixteenth century. Lifelong virginity had become an individual expression of unencumbered self-gift for waiting on the Lord in prayer and charitable service. Marriage, while not the preference among many influential Christian ascetics, nevertheless found favor as the expected path for the majority of Christians to realize their salvation through participation in the divinely-ordered plan of producing and rearing children, and the cultivation of mutually-supportive love between lawful spouses.

Chastity in the Medieval Era

The Continued Exaltation of Virginal Chastity

Despite the edifying thoughts of John Chrysostom and (to a lesser degree) Augustine toward marriage and sexual relations, the exaltation of virginity by influential Christian writers remained throughout the early medieval

---

30. Augustine, *Bon. conj.* 35.

period. Communal celibate monasticism was regarded as the best life to follow for one who truly sought a holy life apart from the cares of the world. Not only unmarried individuals were admitted to monastic life, however; it was not so unusual that married couples who were also drawn to the fullness of monastic life could individually, by mutual consent, embrace lifelong continence and enter respective male and female communities.[31]

By the eighth century, we find the emergence of ecclesiastical attempts to regulate the frequency of marital intercourse. At least three principal justifications emerged for this: The patristic belief that marital intercourse was always the occasion for at least some small degree, or venial sin;[32] the Old Testament-based demand of sexual abstinence for those partaking in ritual sacrifice was adopted to show respect for reception of the Eucharistic sacrifice; and the ever-present ecclesiastical wariness toward the possibility of marital sexual lust. Examining some of the priest-monk collections of "penitential" lists that guided their early practice of individual confession reveals that couples were expected to be abstinent during particular seasons of the liturgical year as well as during certain natural female biological seasons such as menstruation, pregnancy, following childbirth, and during the extended time of lactation.[33] In effect, the available time periods for church-sanctioned physical conjugal relations became significantly curtailed.

High- and Late-Medieval Developments

The twelfth century witnessed a renewed appreciation for an incarnational approach to Christian life and spirituality, that God can and does interact with the human person not only through intellect but also through the senses and moments of human experience (including marital relations). Thinkers such as Bernard of Clairvaux maintained the traditional view that marital sex was also good as a legitimate outlet for sexual urges that might otherwise lead to infidelity and that the sexual relationship served

---

31. Olsen, "Marriage in Barbarian Kingdom and Christian Court," 146–47. This practice was apparently an extension of the earlier-sanctioned Christian practice of "spiritual" or "Josephite" marriages in which couples would agree to follow sexual continence (living as brother and sister) while remaining married.

32. For example, Pope Gregory I specified that if marital intercourse contained any element of pleasure, the sole intent (procreation) had been transgressed and the person had sinned at least venially; the transgression was easily remitted however, when in the service of procreation as the greater good. Gregory the Great, *Pastoral Rule* 3.27.

33. Brundage, *Law, Sex, and Society*, 154–59.

to strengthen the couple's love and affinity for each other; thus, procreation need not be the sole justification for intercourse.[34] Hugh of St. Victor (1096–1141), as Augustine, did not hold that intercourse was a consequence of the first sin but rather a normal part of human existence.[35] Theologically, marriage also was regarded frequently as a visible sign of the relationship of Christ with the church, with intercourse expressing the marvel of the Incarnation. In effect, sexual intercourse brought holiness into a marriage, as Hugh observed:

> Can you find anything else in marriage except conjugal society that makes it sacred and by which you can assert that it is holy? And is it not much more true when two become one in mind than when they become one flesh? If they make each other partner of their flesh and are holy, then if they make each other partners in soul are they not holy? Far be it. They will be two in one flesh, this is a great sacrament; [but I speak] in Christ and in the Church [Eph. 5:31–32].[36]

The growing influence of Scholastic theology also left its mark on the traditional Christian understanding of chastity. Aquinas's *Summa theologica* effectively situated it as subsidiary to the cardinal virtue of temperance. Chastity's aim, he noted, was to govern the sense of touch, specifically in the sexual sphere, as compared to the virtues that regulated food (abstinence) and intoxicating drink (sobriety). Aquinas observed, however, that the fulfilment of sexual desire was unnecessary for individual human survival, unlike the other two. The word *chastity* borrows from that of chastising (curbing) our sexual drive that normally resists our reasoned attempts to guide it.[37] The word may be used in two senses: when referring strictly to the curbing of venereal pleasure, or when speaking of our delight in the pursuit of spiritual union with God through observing the right order of desiring all things as intended for us. Chastity is more directly concerned with the physical exercise of sexual union, while *purity* deals with the proper regulating of behavior (kissing, etc.) that tend to precede union.[38] Lust, contrary to chastity, is the pursuit of sexual pleasure that does not follow one's proper

---

34. Brundage, *Law, Sex, and Society*, 196–99.
35. Pierre, "Marriage, the Body, and Sacrament," 241.
36. Hugh of St. Victor, *Virg.* 1.
37. *Summa* II-II, q. 151, art. 1, ad.
38. *Summa* II-II, q. 151, art. 4, ad.

reasoning according to one's married or celibate state in life.[39] Unlike the earlier prevailing thought, Aquinas held that there was no sin in sexual activity that was rightly-ordered and directed to procreation; the momentary loss of rational control was merely a disordered result of concupiscence.

Chastity in the Modern Era

The events of the Reformation introduced a broader and more tolerant view toward marriage and divorce, along with a lesser one for celibacy, that would challenge the traditionally-accepted standards of behavior in several ways. The first was the reformers' view of marriage itself. While a great good and worthy of God's blessing, they denied any spiritual and sacramental qualities that had been attributed to marriage, and that the practice of virginity offered no greater objective degree of holiness over it. Removing the sacramental nature from marriage also undermined its indissoluble quality, thus marriage should be subject to civil and not ecclesiastical law; a consequence of this was their belief that divorce should be more easily obtainable in the case of failed marriages, with each party possessing the right to remarry.

The second effect on the institution of marriage was the reformers' rejection of procreation as the primary reason for marriage and intercourse, maintaining that marital intercourse was something good and had its worth in nurturing the well-being and spiritual life of the couple. Their belief in the goodness of marital sex also led to a greater recognition of the dignity of women as cocreated by God, serving to counter some of the earlier misogynist thinking from the patristic and medieval eras.[40]

The twenty-fourth session of the Roman Catholic Council of Trent addressed these challenges by reaffirming the traditional teaching on marriage. However, the combined scientific, economic, social, religious, and philosophical evolutions within European society from the seventeenth through nineteenth centuries together exerted tremendous pressures on the traditional understanding of marriage as divinely ordered with a superior procreative intent for physical sexual relations, a topic too complex to adequately explore here but found elsewhere.[41] One evident nineteenth-century result was the growing acceptance of both contraception and

---

39. *Summa* II-II, q. 153, art. 1, ad.
40. Brundage, *Law, Sex, and Society*, 551–61.
41. For instance, read Hitchcock, "Emergence of the Modern Family," 302–31.

abortion, decried by both Roman Catholic and many Protestant religious authorities.[42] Divorce also became more commonly accepted in society with the increasing role of the state in regulating marriage. The stage was set for the contemporary-era challenges and developments in both marital and celibate chastity.

II. TOWARDS A CONTEMPORARY APPRECIATION FOR CHRISTIAN CHASTITY

Wanted—a More Integral Concept of the Human Person

The present-day academic phenomenon of dividing and subdividing fields such as philosophy into ever-more-specialized disciplines has produced one eye-catching subfield known as the "philosophy of sex."[43] One effect is the labeling of various thinkers and authors according to two categories. The first group contains individuals who purportedly ascribed to a "pessimistic" philosophy of sex, including such figures as Augustine of Hippo, Martin Luther, and Immanuel Kant, who tended to regard physical sexual expression as somehow sinful, dangerous, and uncontrollable, to be exercised primarily for the sake of procreation. The second influential group, ranging from Plato (according to some of his works) to the twentieth-century thinker Bertrand Russell, are considered to have held a more "optimistic" and unfettered regard toward sexuality, considered as worthwhile for its own sake, to be enjoyed with little if any moral consequence, and free of historically-conditioned guilt.

Both "pessimistic" and "optimistic" positions tend to address human sexuality in incomplete ways. Neither are conducive to an integrated spiritual-psychological-physical understanding of personhood capable of holding a view of the human person as not only a created being, but also a unique one within the wider realm of creation. The contemporary western secular view of sexuality tends to isolate the human physical sexual dimension from the overall human person, supporting an ethical foundation for human sexuality and reproduction that can be interpreted to justify such activities as abortion-on-demand at any gestation stage for the sake of expediency, same-sex marriages, and gender-reassignment surgery. At least one writer has recognized a contemporary tendency to deconstruct

---

42. Hitchcock, "Emergence of the Modern Family," 321–22.
43. Soble, "Philosophy of Sexuality."

the integral human person into separate components of body-mind-spirit that has enkindled yet a new form of the earlier-mentioned Gnosticism. Once again, the spiritual-mental perception of reality becomes the primary determinant of reality, leading to antagonism between the spiritual and physical realms of physical creation, including the human body.[44]

While historical Christianity may justly incur contemporary criticism for some of its past views toward human sexuality, the Roman Catholic tradition in recent years has embraced a more integral view of the human person as a spiritual, thinking, feeling, and sensate being whose ingrained sexuality, including the capacity for physical sexual expression, is both a sacred gift and responsibility. From this more optimistic perspective, one's sexuality is an integral part of the person through which one is capable of collaborating in the ongoing divine work of creation. One must always keep in mind, though, the great loving and creative potential of sex that can also be abused and become an instrument of evil.

Twentieth-Century Christian Developments

In answer to the growing acceptance and promotion of artificial conception and abortion, the Roman Catholic Church consistently has condemned practices that tended to separate human sexuality and sexual intercourse from its primary and sacred end of procreation. Pope Pius XI did so in his 1930 encyclical *Casti Connubi* (On Chaste Marriage). His successor Pius XII reiterated these views in a 1951 address to Italian midwives and in a 1956 document addressing the second World Congress of Fertility and Sterility, denouncing the latter group's organized efforts to promote artificial contraception and the limitation of births for the sake of economic development. Despite the influential works of Dietrich von Hildebrand (in English, *Marriage*, 1929) and Herbert Doms (*The Meaning of Marriage*, 1939), both suggesting a broader vision of marriage in service to the couple within a Christian context, there was little if any reconsideration of the traditional Roman perspective toward marriage and conjugal chastity until the Second Vatican Council.

The 1965 papal encyclical on the role of the Christian church in the modern world opened the door to a broader vision for marriage and marital intercourse. While still recognizing that the primary end of marriage was to provide an environment for welcoming children and forming them

44. George, "Gnostic Liberalism," 33–38.

in a family rooted in daily self-giving acts of charity, the document gave equal importance to the two main reasons for marriage as both unitive (for the sake of the couple) and procreative, both of which intended to integrate into a holy way of life:

> Marriage to be sure is not instituted solely for procreation; rather, its very nature as an unbreakable compact between persons, and the welfare of the children, both demand that the mutual love of the spouses be embodied in a rightly ordered manner, that it grow and ripen. Therefore, marriage persists as a whole manner and communion of life, and maintains its value and indissolubility, even when despite the often intense desire of the couple, offspring are lacking.[45]

The document thus rearticulated the traditional view of marriage that had previously given greater weight to its place for the procreation and education of children, in the context of supporting and fostering greater spousal love. This contemporary view has been developed further in subsequent decades, most notably among the writings of Pope John Paul II and his "theology of the body" that honors the spousal intimacy, love, and joy of sex that a couple will naturally experience as part of their shared love, while reminding couples that love is meant to be a reflection of the divine love calling each spouse to an ever-deeper gift of self for the sake of the other. Such self-giving love calls the Christian couple to a trusting relationship with each other and with Christ, considered as the third presence in their marriage and evident in the quality of their shared love. Such a totally self-giving spousal love, if it is to mature, must be open to the possible creation of new life through avoiding the use of artificial contraceptive practices.

The Second Vatican Council also repeated the Roman Catholic Church's timeless appreciation for committed celibacy, recognizing it as a more complete way to give oneself completely to God with undivided heart to prayer and service. One does not casually embrace this life; rather, it is possible only for individuals who are strengthened through divine grace to follow it.[46] Following the way of celibacy is a special way to foster union with God:

> The chastity of celibates and virgins, as a manifestation of dedication to God with an undivided heart (cf. 1 Cor 7:32–34), is a reflection of the infinite love which links the three Divine Persons in the

---

45. Paul VI, *Gaudium et Spes*, no. 50.
46. Paul VI, *Lumen Gentium*, no. 42c.

mysterious depths of the life of the Trinity, the love to which the Incarnate Word bears witness even to the point of giving his life, the love "poured into our hearts through the Holy Spirit" (Rom 5:5), which evokes a response of total love for God and the brethren.[47]

The 1964 Vatican II document on the mystery of the church also recognized the spiritual fruitfulness and dedicated charity that is possible in lifelong celibacy:

Likewise, the holiness of the Church is fostered in a special way by the observance of the counsels proposed in the Gospel by Jesus to his disciples. An eminent position among these is held by virginity or the celibate state. This is a precious gift of divine grace given by the Father to certain souls, whereby they may devote themselves to God alone the more easily, due to an undivided heart. This perfect continency, out of desire for the kingdom of heaven, has always been held in particular honor in the Church. The reason for this was and is that perfect continency for the love of God is an incentive to charity, and is certainly a particular source of spiritual fecundity in the world.[48]

Christian Chastity in Relationships with God, with Others, and as Part of Creation[49]

How might we articulate a contemporary vision for cultivating the virtue of chastity among Christian disciples that honors the integrity of the person and the gift of sexuality that he or she has received?

With God

The Christian tradition attests to the presence of certain profound qualities within the human person; three of these stand out in particular. Each person possesses an *innate dignity* from a loving God who has imbued that unique person with the appropriate sexuality appropriate to a male or female, inseparable from his or her personhood, shaping how that person relates to others and the surrounding world. As a person, I have been created

---

47. John Paul II, *Vita Consecrata*, no. 21.
48. Paul VI, *Lumen Gentium*, no. 42c.
49. The work of Vincent Genovesi, SJ was helpful in forming this synthesis. Genovesi, "Sexuality," 947–54.

to live as one held in God's love, to respond with my life to God's love and to allow this divine love to guide me, ultimately to realize the deepest union with God's love. Likewise, I have been created as a *relational* person who is capable of loving others in relationship, both with God and with other persons, however imperfectly, always influenced by the gift of my sexuality to ever more fully love others with God's own love, a self-giving love that ultimately has no limit. God has also made me as a *creative* person. I have been formed with the ability to create, to participate materially (even if unwittingly) in God's expansive ongoing act of creation; whether through creating works of art or other material objects, conceiving scientific theories or organizational structures, forming human communities with other people, nurturing the deep self-giving love that forms a covenant-based family setting, or uniting with a sexually complementary other to create another human being.

With Others

Following Jesus' teaching to "love one another as I have loved you" (John 15:12), Christian disciples are called to love one another with the fathomless love of Christ, a demanding lifelong project of refining one's love through relinquishing self-centeredness, with the end of realizing an ever-deeper love for others. My inner drive to relate to others comes from the depth of my personhood that has experienced God's love, expressing itself through my individual personality with its traits, mannerisms, and ways of relating to the world around me that are shaped and accented by my inherent sexual nature as female or male. In fact, each of us is influenced by both gender possibilities and retain qualities of both, but one will predominate.

My gender-based sexuality will also shape my particular way of sharing God's love in relationships with others, seeking to express itself according to the various depths of loving friendship that I encounter throughout my lifetime. My determined gender as male or female that I received before birth is also a continual reminder that, while I am created with the possibility of physical union with another, I am a single autonomous being who is incomplete by myself. My inner drive for transcendence reaches out continually in love, however imperfectly, both to God and to all others as God loves them. Its fullest (though always incomplete) potential for human fulfilment is found through a loving union of total self-gift to a person of the opposite sex with whom I have discovered a mutual love, and to whom

Chastity Leading to Deeper Christian Love

I am compelled to pledge my future for the rest of my life in the committed state of matrimony. It is in this lifelong state that I am most fully able to give of myself to another person spiritually and bodily. The love that I may share with a committed spouse finds its source in God's love for us. This love is potentially limitless and is meant to be fruitful in all aspects of our life, calling forth from both of us daily acts of self-denial in matters great and small in loving service of my spouse and family, ultimately for the sake of finding one's eternal happiness through the perfected love that can result.

The physical experience of sexual intercourse engenders most deeply the notion of two complementarily-sexed human beings in the act of "two becoming one." Sexual intercourse within committed matrimony is meant to be the locus for deepest physical giving of one spouse to the other, a symbol of the total-gift of Jesus' love for God's people. This self-giving love is meant to be fruitful in many dimensions of marriage, including the possible fruitfulness of another human life.

As Christians, our loving relationship with God will naturally induce us to glorify God through different outlets along the particular pathway of our individual lives. A question I might ask is: Does the exercise of my overall creative activity glorify God? Unlike other animals, we are gifted with rational and reflective abilities, including the ability to choose based on informed reason and self-knowledge rather than merely following instinct or sensual pleasure. How might I best participate in creation? Perhaps that will include exercising my sexuality in the self-giving commitment of marriage and, if we are open to God's creative plan, ordinarily through the creation and rearing of children. As continent unmarried persons, we may temporarily refrain from the deeply-expressed sexuality appropriate to those in a married commitment to better prepare and educate ourselves for a future career. We may also desire to give space for a still-new loving relationship to mature, perhaps destined for marriage but not yet ready for a life of totally-committed self-giving of marriage and family life, the most protective setting for the vulnerability that sharing the total mutual self-gift of sexual intercourse demands and deserves.

The loving potential of our sexuality might also move us to dedicate our lives, in love, for the sake of another great good that precludes marriage and physical expression. Do we perhaps find our best spiritual harmony in following Christ with a whole heart through a life of committed celibacy, offering many possible ways to seek God in daily life through prayer and charitable service of some kind? Maybe we're moved to refrain from physical sexual expression for a specific period, even for the rest of our life, for the sake of ministry or another form of self-giving such as caring for an elderly parent or another person who needs the generous and perhaps extended attention that only we can provide.

Each of these ways engages us as sexual beings, physically or not, in calling forth ongoing expressions of love that is a reflection, however imperfect, of the divine love.

As a Cocreative Part of Creation

God's creation is continually unfolding through time. Human beings, created beings that we are, influence and contribute to the created world around us for good or for ill. Save for humans, all of creation naturally glorifies the Creator by force of their very being. Trees grow from saplings into mature wonders of innumerable kinds, sizes, and foliage, glorifying God through their normal life progression according to the divine design, even in their eventual death and decomposition that serve to nurture the emergence of new life. Animals of whatever species likewise point to the majesty and diverse beauty of their Creator, whether by way of one's beautiful fur coat or reptilian skin design, another's effortless leaping, or the superhuman strength of a third.

Human beings likewise can best glorify God through their lives when lived as true persons who are conscious of their God-given dignity. Such individuals can more freely allow themselves to be guided by the loving intent of the Creator that has loved them into being and made them capable of sharing more and more fully this divine love with others, while aided and guided by our affective and rational abilities. We do this while integrating our sexuality that permeates us and is at our service to be exercised responsibly, calling for the restraint of chastity according to our particular way of Christian discipleship. With a healthy and unselfish sexuality, guided by chastity, we are capable of accomplishing wonderful things in harmony with the divine plan. Without an effective virtue of chastity, our lives will likely become dissipated; at worst, its absence can lead to the destruction of ourselves, our relationships, to the detriment of society and even the world around us.

A healthy and effective virtue of chastity, and our respect for the potential of love that we can realize through it, will also foster our respect for not only human life but for all life. Allowing our lives to be inordinately defined by an exaggerated need for sex moves us away from a properly-ordered view of our lives into the realm of self-centeredness. In this latter stance, life beyond ourselves can become merely instrumental for our selfish ends while losing sight of its divine source and intention for authentic human love. Pope Francis warns against this in *Laudato Si'*: "When we fail to acknowledge as part of reality the worth of a poor person, a human embryo, a person with disabilities—to offer just a few examples—it becomes difficult to hear the cry of nature itself; everything is connected."[50]

Our personal attitude toward the miracle of human life and the exercise of chastity does not remain at the level of the individual; it ripples outward through the level of family, affecting society and ultimately the wider created world that we, too, occupy and share with each other as co-created beings.

---

50. Francis, *Laudato Si'*, no. 117.

5

Voluntary Poverty for Greater Availability to the Spirit

CHRISTIAN EVANGELICAL OR VOLUNTARY poverty as a spiritually liberating practice has been a perennial ideal for Christian disciples from the time of Jesus and his first followers. Today, though, it can easily be misunderstood for at least two reasons. One is that *voluntary* poverty can often be confused with the actual condition of material poverty that plagues so much of the world. Disciples for the reign of God consider this latter type of poverty, wherever it exists, as an evil condition to be confronted and transformed according to the values of the reign of God that they struggle to bring into full reality. Another cause for misunderstanding evangelical poverty is due to the inconsistent practice of both church and Christian disciples to "live in the world but not of it." For example, critics of the Roman Catholic Church will point to its perceived wealth in artwork and other pieces of its sizable patrimony, even as the church gives a voice to the economically poor and promotes extensive programs to alleviate the condition and its consequences.

Long considered as an evangelical "counsel" for Christian disciples to cultivate in imitation of Jesus' earthly life, all Christian disciples are exhorted to practice evangelical poverty within the constraints of their particular way of life. Members of consecrated religious communities vow themselves to observe the virtue in a more radical form so that they may more freely follow in the footsteps of Jesus who lived poorly and detached from all possession, desiring to offer life examples that point beyond themselves to the One whom they follow. All other baptized Christians, though not bound

Voluntary Poverty for Greater Availability to the Spirit

to observe evangelical poverty to the same degree as vowed religious, are nonetheless exhorted to let themselves be guided by it as a ssuitable way to live between the two extreme attitudes of prodigality (reckless spending on oneself) and miserliness.

There have been various traditional reasons for exhorting the practice of voluntary poverty among Christians in response to cultural, social, and institutional concerns over the centuries. As we shall find, several of them continue to strike a resonant chord in our contemporary day.

I. CHRISTIAN VOLUNTARY POVERTY THROUGH THE CENTURIES

Voluntary Poverty in Scripture

Old Testament

Poverty freely embraced as a religious ideal was a strange notion among the early Jews. To be poor was generally considered to be an undesirable plight, with the poor collectively regarded as indigent, humiliated, deprived, and subject to unjust treatment by others. One's actual condition of material poverty was viewed as a sign of divine disfavor for the person or group of individuals, likely incurred for not having lived according to the Jewish law, as contrasted with those who did.[1] However, the Jewish prophets exhorted the people of Israel to be sensitive to the daily plight of the poor and seek to alleviate their hardship, whatever may have been the reason for their condition, proclaiming that God had a particular sympathy toward those in need.[2]

The exilic and post-exilic periods witnessed a transformation in understanding about what it meant to be considered among the poor, with a link developing between actual material poverty and an interior quality called "poverty of spirit," desirable among those who sought to be closer to God. Those who were poor also would possess the spiritual characteristics of the poor, by necessity being more dependent upon God's goodness in their states of humility and vulnerability. Because of this, the materially poor were seen to have an advantage in their relationship with God, while the more advantaged were prone to slip into indifference and seek their

---

1. See, for instance, Pss 1:3 & 112:3.
2. Wilcock, "Poor, The," 1732. See also Stenzel, "Poverty," 671–73.

security in material gain rather than in their relationship with a providential God. Personal riches did not automatically discount one from a just relationship with God but did present a more challenging road so to avoid any interior hardness of heart; voluntary poverty thus came to be considered as an essential quality for growth in faithfulness to God. The Jewish Essenes of the inter-testamental period chose voluntary material poverty in service to sharing of material goods, in part to avoid the sinful snares of material possession.[3]

New Testament

The interpretation of poverty as spiritual poverty predominates in the writings of the New Testament, offering several reasons why personal poverty is preferable to wealth. For instance, Luke presents Jesus' teaching through parables such as Lazarus and the rich man (16:19–30) and other images, such as "it is easier for a camel to pass through the eye of a needle than for a rich person to enter the kingdom of God" (18:25), so to reveal the difficulty that accompanied wealth and possessions. These views resonated with the earlier Jewish prophetic admonition that material riches tended to impede one's fuller relationship with God. Both synoptic renditions of the Beatitudes ("Blessed are the poor in spirit" of Matthew 5:3 and "Blessed are you who are poor" in Luke 6:20) signal that to fully live in the reign of God required personal freedom from the snares of material possession and an active dependence on God's providential love. There is little evangelical support for some theological interpretations that Jesus eschewed personal wealth or possessions, considering that both Luke and John portray Jesus in such moments as visiting the Bethany home of Lazarus and his sisters and dining with other individuals of means. Jesus' point seemed rather to be that material possessions tended to impede a disciple from entering and participating more fully and freely in the Reign of God.

Jesus' adaptation of the prophetic teaching on poverty was total and yet voluntary. He did not impose the discipline on his followers, though he instructed his apostles to practice it in their itinerant ministry of preaching repentance. They were also to go beyond a "poverty in spirit" to one that was physically and visibly evident, with two notable consequences. First, disciples so living would be led to depend upon God's loving providence in their regard (Matt 6:25–34) and so be free to follow Jesus. Jesus gave

3. Mulhern, *Dedicated Poverty*, 9.

Voluntary Poverty for Greater Availability to the Spirit

the lived example of the poor one who depended on his Father's loving care for him (Matt 8:20), who dispossessed himself of both his divinity and ultimately of his human life (Phil 2:5–8) in faithfulness and radical submission to his Father's providential love for all people. Second, the practice of voluntary poverty should also produce in disciples an attitude of generosity, with a willingness to share what they had with people in need.[4]

Jesus also taught that concern for one's neighbor was a consequence for being brothers and sisters of the same Creator. Salvation was not exclusively the prerogative of the materially poor. In order to realize the fullness of life, rich and poor alike needed to realize an attitude of detachment from material possessions, to be made visible through a willingness to share from one's possessions to the extent of sharing from what one needed to subsist, as illustrated by the instance of the poor widow giving from her necessity (Mark 12:41–44).

The Acts of the Apostles describes the community of Jerusalem that arose in the first years after Jesus' resurrection and has held a special place throughout the history of Christian spirituality. Gathered together following the Pentecost fervor from Jesus' first disciples, the community was blessed with many converts who accepted the gospel. Its members pooled together and shared their economic resources; they "were together and had all things in common; they would sell their possessions and goods and distribute the proceeds to all, as any had need" (Acts 2:44–45). While the Pauline letters and other texts give evidence that there were people of property and wealth who were among the first Christians, it is commonly accepted that the early body of the church was made up largely of the materially poor. The great number of converts meant that the Jerusalem community resources would have been challenged to meet the essential needs of so many. The apostle Paul sought funds for this cherished community and beseeched other Christian centers such as Antioch (Acts 11:27–30) to support this favored group. As important as this community was to the early Christians, the intensively "communistic" modality of the Jerusalem Christian community receives scant if any mention in later Christian communities.

The Epistle of James, sometimes presented as a rebuke to those Christians who were materially blessed, more likely sought to restore community harmony among both poor and wealthy among the Jewish-Christian communities. The letter exhorts those who lacked financial standing to see that the grace of their lowliness was of greater merit (Jas 1:9–11); at the same

---

4. Balthasar, "Poverty of Christ," 196–98.

time, the wealthy should concern themselves to live while guided by a desire to please God and not in conformity to social mores (4:1–10). Business transactions should always be tempered by a concern to live justly as God intends and to treat others likewise (4:17—5:6). The letter reiterates the earliest Christian belief that material wealth can sway individuals from following the path of new life which had been opened by the poor and risen Christ. We find that the author is concerned for the deleterious effect that material wealth can have, both for its possessors whose hearts may become hardened and for the less fortunate who may fall prey to envy and resentment.

Christian Poverty in the Patristic Era

The Church Fathers

The early Christian attitude toward poverty became reinforced by strains of Greek philosophy that placed a preference for the spiritual dimension of one's life over material goods and riches. This helped lead more affluent persons who struggled with the literal interpretation of Jesus' words that it is easier for a camel to pass through the eye of a needle than for a rich one to enter the kingdom of God (Matt 19:24) and other early Christian readings that challenged their ability to find salvation.

Clement of Alexandria instructed in his sermon "Who Is the Rich Man that Shall Be Saved?" that one's interior detachment from possessions by rich and poor alike was necessary for salvation, while underscoring that the materially poor were the special friends of God. Clement also taught that individuals of means had a privileged way to seek God's favor through using their riches in service to alleviate the suffering of the poor. The more wealthy Christians were thus acting as agents of Christ as well as winning the favor of the poor who had God's special preference. One could therefore practice almsgiving as a powerful penitential expression, since charitable and free sharing of goods would help to win God's favor.[5]

In his work *On the Dress of Virgins*, Cyprian of Carthage stressed that the exterior apparel of women following this vocation should reflect an inner modesty and freedom from the advantages of any personal wealth:

> You say that you are wealthy and rich and you think that you must use those things which God has wished you to possess. Use them, certainly, but for the things of salvation . . . Let the poor feel that

5. Weaver, "Wealth and Poverty," 371.

you are wealthy; let the needy feel that you are rich. Lend your estate to God; give food to Christ . . . For in this very matter you are sinning against God, if you think that riches were given to you by Him for this purpose, to enjoy them thoroughly without a view of salvation.[6]

Cyprian's initial attitude toward Christians and excessive wealth followed the more conciliatory and inviting tones of Clement. Cyprian became more severe following a period of Roman persecution, however, observing that many Christians had turned away from the demands of their faith from fear of losing their wealth. His treatise *On the Lapsed* interpreted the sufferings of persecution as God's judgment upon those wealthy who had grown slack in their faith due to avarice:

> The truth, brethren, must not be concealed, nor must the matter and cause of our wound be kept silent. Blind love of one's personal property has deceived many; nor could they have been prepared or ready for departing, when their possessions bound them like fetters. Those fetters were for those who remained, those chains by which virtue was retarded, and faith hard pressed, and mind bound, and the soul imprisoned, so that they who clung to earthly things became as booty and food for the serpent who, according to the words of God, devours the earth.[7]

In this second work, Cyprian endorsed another reason for the practice of almsgiving, regarding it as a way for them to atone for their past sinfulness and avoid the penalties awaiting them at the final judgement.[8]

John Chrysostom followed this attitude in the wake of the fourth-century legalization of Christianity. Imperial favor had greatly diminished the church dependence on wealthy donors to meet the needs of the poor, resulting in the loss of a traditional outlet for charity and for cultivating detachment. A man who was aware that possessions could easily become a stumbling block for Christians, Chrysostom addressed in several works the new danger of apathy among Christians of means. His sermon on Lazarus and the rich man (Luke 16:19–31) underscored the fate that awaited those who grew in indifference toward the needy and, conversely, the eternal benefit of repenting in this life.

---

6. Cyprian, *Hab. virg.* 11.
7. Cyprian, *Laps.* 11.
8. Cyprian, *Laps.* 35.

From Strength to Strength

The new freedom of Christianity from persecution and marginalization, while a blessing, also brought a relaxed coexistence with the surrounding pagan cultures and growing moral laxity within the Christian community. It helped to nurture the attraction of some toward the newly-developing Christian primitive monasticism, becoming accepted as the continuation of the apostolic lifestyle and as a significant way to practice voluntary poverty. Athanasius of Alexandria (296–373) relates in his *Life of Anthony* (of Egypt) how the youth sold his possessions and took to the wilderness upon hearing Jesus' words to "sell all that you own and distribute the money to the poor . . . then come, follow me" (Luke 18:22) and relied on divine providence for his daily needs.[9] The collected wisdom of the monastic desert elders (the *Apophthegms of the Fathers*) contains many exhortations for embracing voluntary poverty as essential to achieve detachment from possessions, considered essential for experiencing God in the desert. At least some women also followed this path; one was Melanie the Elder (342–410) who gave away her considerable Roman wealth and went into the desert, eventually inspiring her affluent granddaughter and family to leave behind their possessions and comfortable lifestyle.[10]

During the later third- and early fourth-century period, Basil of Caesarea (330–379) lived for some time as a monk but eventually was elected as bishop. For much of his life, he showed a particular sympathy for the plight of the poor who suffered due to a number of social and agricultural hardships. He maintained that all men and women were called to grow in their intercommunion with each other and with Christ, so to realize their fullness of life as a son or daughter of God.

Being a follower of Christ calls a disciple to obey not only the first commandment of the Decalogue, to love the Lord with one's whole heart, soul, and mind; but also the second, to love one's neighbor as oneself. To this end, Basil taught that the poor must not be denied their basic needs by members of the more wealthy class, who should be generous in distributing their excess for the sake of the needy. Basil set an example with his own life and inheritance, using it to buy food and establishing other services for those in need.[11] Also, his sermons did not hesitate to use direct and

---

9. Athanasius, *Vit. Ant.* 2–3.

10. Palladius, *Lausiac History* 54. The work also recounts other women who were revered for their desert asceticism, including Sylvania (*Lausiac History* 55), Olympia (*Lausiac History* 56), and Candida and Gelasia (*Lausiac History* 57).

11. Siepierski, "Poverty and Spirituality," 321–26.

Voluntary Poverty for Greater Availability to the Spirit

challenging words to rouse his wealthy and indifferent listeners, such as one concerning the rich young man of Matthew's Gospel:

> It is thus evident that you are far from fulfilling the commandment, and that you bear false witness within your own soul that you have loved your neighbor as yourself... For if what you say is true, that you have kept from your youth the commandment of love and have given to everyone the same as to yourself, then how did you come by this abundance of wealth? Care for the needy requires the expenditure of wealth: when all share alike, disbursing their possessions among themselves, they each receive a small portion for their individual needs. Thus, those who love their neighbor as themselves possess nothing more than their neighbor; yet surely, you seem to have great possessions!... For the more you abound in wealth, the more you lack in love.[12]

He also taught that human society existed for a holy purpose, to facilitate the growth and flourishing of its members; anything that impeded this, particularly as it affected its poorer and marginalized members, was to be rooted out. A good example was during periods of drought or famine, when those of wealth were able to stave off hunger and suffering while the poor lived in anguish. While Basil called the rich to make available their stored food for the sake of the poor, he also challenged the poor to alleviate the need of others who were less endowed:

> Are you poor? You know someone who is even poorer. You have provisions for only ten days, but someone else has only enough for one day. As a good and generous person, redistribute your surplus to the needy. Do not shrink from giving the little that you have; do not prefer your own benefit to remedying the common distress... And when you have thus spoken and acted, the bread you have given from your straitened circumstances will become seed for sowing that bears a rich harvest, a promise of food, an envoy of mercy.[13]

The emerging Western Christian view came to echo that of the East, observing the role of charity through disbursing one's possessions to alleviate the needs of others rather than amassing them for oneself. Jerome defended the tradition of voluntary poverty in a scathing missive against the antagonist Vigilantius who had been critical of several ministerial practices, referring to the apostle Paul who had continually requested aid in

---

12. See Basil of Caesarea, *On Social Justice*, 43, in his sermon on Matthew 19:16–22.
13. See Basil of Caesarea, *On Social Justice*, 83, in his sermon on Amos 3:8.

the name of the early Jerusalem Christians. Jerome wrote that a disciple must not be overly attached to possessions but rather should follow Jesus' instruction to "sell all that you own and distribute the money to the poor ... then come, follow me (Luke 18:22)."[14] Those people doing so could hope for God's mercy through the prayers of the poor whom they assisted, God's favored ones.

Augustine of Hippo promoted a patristic teaching that one's wealth, indeed whatever one has, originally belongs to God and is a gift to the possessor; any unneeded surplus should be returned to God through giving it to those in need: "Ask yourself how much he has given you and then pick out what you need; all the rest of your things lie there as superfluities, but for other people they are necessities. The superfluity of the rich is necessary to the poor. If you hold onto superfluous items, then, you are keeping what belongs to someone else."[15]

Exhortations to practice voluntary poverty frequently appear in works dealing with both supporting vocations to consecrated virginity and also as an edifying practice for clergy. For the latter, observing personal poverty helped to serve as a foil to the clerical temptations to avarice and seeking personal social advantage, and was meant to offer an edifying example in the lives of those who were ordained to serve and not be served. Augustine stands out as the architect of a form of communal life that he followed together with his clergy, living together within the episcopal residence while guided by a version of what is traditionally called the *Rule of Augustine*. Their common life followed that of a monastic community in many ways, while not following the typical monastic life of separation from the world. Augustine's sense of voluntary poverty was an essential element that fostered among his clergy the Jerusalem community ideal of "one heart and one mind," serving both as a community goal and a form of witness to the power of the Christian gospel message amid the declining Roman Empire.[16] Augustine insisted that his clergy should follow blameless lives with regard to any wealth that might accrue to them through their ministry, offering instead a public witness of their simplicity through uniformity in dress and limited possessions. The influence of Augustine's rule would recede for several hundred years until its reemergence in the tenth-century rules for cathedral canon communities.

14. Jerome, *Vigil.* 14.
15. Augustine, *Ennerat. Ps.* 147.
16. Van Bavel, "Evangelical Inspiration of the Rule of St. Augustine," 83.

Voluntary Poverty for Greater Availability to the Spirit

Early Western Monasticism

The emergence of monasticism in fourth-century Western Europe helped to solidify the practice of evangelical poverty in the early Christian spiritual tradition. The fifth-century ascetic John Cassian reacted to the growing moral laxity among Christians who merely assented to the teachings of Jesus without exhibiting any exterior proof of detachment from material goods. His two great collections of Eastern monastic heritage were in part concerned to introduce the discipline in the West while providing an early interpretation of the early teaching of Jesus and the first apostles, but Cassian's thought has also influenced the wider Christian spirituality tradition. The seventh book of his *Institutes* considers the sin of avarice with which monks had to struggle in order to reach the fullness of Christian life, noting three basic types of monks. The first is when monks begin to inordinately enjoy and hoard the goods of their new lifestyle that they never possessed before. The second and third types were more a danger to those from privileged backgrounds who had embraced the ascetical life: They could either grow weary of their simpler state in life and develop a desire to return to their more privileged ways, or in the case of monks who had never really left behind their attachments upon beginning their ascetical way.[17]

The sixth-century monastic rule of Benedict, which eventually became the dominant expression of Western communal monastic life, described any monastic practice of personal ownership as a vice that ultimately would prove injurious to the communal and interdependent nature of Benedictine life.[18] While there is little overt treatment of voluntary poverty in the Benedictine rule, both physical and interior detachment were indispensable to a monk's life and found their expression in day-to-day observance of the rule through practices such as seeking permission to accept gifts, cultivating an attitude of spiritual indifference toward their abbot, and having a dependence upon the monastery for all of their needs. They were also expected to exercise an attitude of stewardship toward community items, noting that material goods such as tools were to be used and treated with care; individuals who failed to do so were to be reprimanded.[19] The resilience of this spirit within Benedictine life would inspire the monastic

---

17. Goodrich, "John Cassian on Monastic Poverty," 303–4.
18. RB 33.
19. RB 32.

foundation of Cluny and other reform communities that renewed their attitude and practice of voluntary poverty and detachment.

Celtic monasticism was very much a part of ordinary church hierarchical life and governance; the few remaining Celtic monastic rules reveal a fierceness in its observance in order to stamp out any development of avarice. The fourth chapter of the rule of Saint Columbanus warns that monks should beware of falling into covetousness, comparing it to leprosy and the sin through which Judas betrayed Christ. Voluntary poverty will aid the monk to develop a inner spiritual poverty and renouncement that will move one from disdain for possessions through a liberation from all vice, until the monk finds a perfect love for God and for divine things.

Christian Poverty in the High- and Late-Medieval Periods

A Growing Zeal to Imitate the Poor Jesus of the Gospels

Among the medieval clergy who were not members of religious orders, we have only limited ability as to their practice of evangelical poverty before the twelfth century, apart from considering various attempts to reform their wider spiritual and moral lives. Concern for an edifying and supportive lifestyle for priests included attempts to impose the Benedictine rule on clergy, with limited success. The adoption of the rule of Augustine, along with following a life in common as canons attached to a cathedral or other common residence, provided both greater success and more pastoral flexibility. These canon communities, which initially had a feminine counterpart such as the community founded by Saint Brigid of Ireland (d. ca. 525), also regulated times for common prayer, uniform dress, and life outside the community. The additional practice of combining individual incomes into a common fund sought to correct a tendency for communities to become internally divided according to economic status between its members of greater financial resources, who were able to enjoy a more comfortable living reality, and those of lesser means.

By the twelfth century, there was a growing recognition among Christian faithful that many of the clergy had drifted far from the Gospel portrayals of Jesus and the apostles as itinerant and poor men who relied on God's loving providence for daily needs. Clerical practices such as simony (the buying and selling of ecclesiastical office or blessings) and a concern of many priests to financially provide for offspring instigated the development

Voluntary Poverty for Greater Availability to the Spirit

of lay preaching movements who strove to follow a more evangelical lifestyle such as the *humiliati* and the consecrated life institutions founded by Francis of Assisi (1181/2–1226) and Dominic of Guzman (ca. 1170–1221). More serious challenges to ecclesiastical authority emerged among the followers of John Hus (1374–1415) and those of the Waldensians, whose movements were largely reactions to church ministers who had strayed far from the Gospel ideal of detachment from wealth. These diverse movements shared at least one common element—the recognition that their ministry of vocal preaching and instruction needed to be fortified with personal witness through an evangelical lifestyle of voluntary poverty and detachment from concerns over wealth and security, following the example of Jesus and the Twelve. Church efforts to stem economic corruption and encourage its ministers to holiness led also to the Gregorian reform and the four influential Lateran councils that imposed many reforms during the later twelfth and thirteenth centuries.

The Gospel ideal of evangelical poverty also captivated the interest of many laypersons who desired to follow it within a supportive community lifestyle, while not being canonically and permanently bound to them. The *humiliati* continued in existence through the fourteenth century, an eventual victim of its association with what was considered an ecclesiastically unorthodox group. Other lay communities appeared during this time, most notably the male Beghards and the female Beguines of the so-called "Low Countries" (including present-day Belgium and Holland), whose common simple life was based on shared manual work, prayer, and gospel poverty. Many women of means gave up their personal wealth for the sake of following Christ more closely in this way.[20]

Other lay men and women who desired to follow the Christian way with a greater spirit of voluntary poverty found encouragement and support through the emerging system of Franciscan and other lay third-order associations and parish confraternities. Lay groups associated with religious orders struggled against ecclesiastical efforts to regulate them in lifestyles more akin to consecrated religious life. Two outstanding example of this supportive way to live the detachment of mendicant life are found in the lives of the thirteenth century Clare of Assisi (1194–1253), who shunned her wealth so to follow the way of her mentor Francis, and the fourteenth-century lay Dominican Catherine of Siena (1347–1461).

---

20. Baker, *Medieval Women*, 260.

From Strength to Strength

Christian Poverty in the Modern Era

Martin Luther (1483–1546) challenged the traditional Christian theology that understood gospel poverty as necessary for the salvation of the wealthy through the practice of almsgiving. Luther's understanding of justification by grace alone precluded any practice that sought justification through merit, including those who sought God's favor by giving to the poor in the hope that they would win God's favor. For Luther, any theological enterprise should lead to a pastoral end; any charitable giving to those in need should be justified in terms of meeting a social or pastoral need and never as a way to gain salvation. The prevailing Christian belief that poverty was a state favored by God and that the poor could be used by the rich to be saved were, in effect, a systemic means for allowing the poor to remain poor, for Christians to largely ignore their plight, and causing the perpetuation of a social ill.[21]

The fifteenth and sixteenth centuries witnessed several efforts in Spain, France, and Italy to foster necessary Roman Catholic reform; one chief means of which was through reform of the clergy. By the sixteenth century, groups of *oratori* comprising both laity and clergy sprang up through the inspiration of Philip Neri (1515–95). His joyful and attractive spirituality effectively encouraged Oratory members to follow a more committed Christian lay vocation through encouragement in prayer, devotion, and service. Neri, first in his years as adult layman and later as priest, was an effective example of a disciple who observed a radical evangelical poverty through depending on divine providence for his needs; he also exhorted his followers to follow his example and give away any surplus wealth to the poor at Christmastime.[22]

The seventeenth-century version of the Bérullian "French School" of spirituality also focused heavily on clergy reform as an essential component. Olier, in his *Introduction to the Christian Life and Virtues*, offered meditations on several virtues and qualities of Catholic disciples to cultivate as part of a disciple's overarching goal of becoming an all-embracing act of religious offering to God through interiorizing specific virtues and other qualities of Jesus. The eleventh chapter offers a treatise on voluntary poverty that explores its double purpose; as a remedy for our human tendency to become overly attached to material possessions, and to foster an interior

---

21. Lindberg, "Luther on Poverty," 85–92.
22. Miller, "Saint Philip Neri and the Priesthood," 13.

state of desiring union with God as the only worthwhile possession. Whatever good experienced in created things was minuscule in relationship to the divine Good that is its source. Olier also taught that practicing evangelical poverty could also serve as a penitential practice, to atone for whatever sinful use that one had made of created goods.[23]

At the dawn of the twentieth century, we find that several traditional reasons for the practice of evangelical poverty have persisted through the preceding centuries, such as to more freely follow the way of Christ; to give visible witness to the gospel message; as a way to cultivate an inner spirit of poverty; and as a penitential expression through almsgiving. Some of these continue to find a worthy hearing in the contemporary era.

II. TOWARDS A CONTEMPORARY APPRECIATION OF CHRISTIAN POVERTY

Following the innovations of Vatican II, Christian spiritual life in the Roman Catholic tradition has changed considerably from what existed in earlier centuries. This has come about through the rediscovered focus on the incarnational nature of Jesus; a greater recognition that he calls us to address the various forms of both spiritual and physical suffering in other people, especially the poor; an increasing openness to the world and societal needs; and growing involvement of Christian lay faithful (i.e., neither ordained nor publically vowed) in church mission and ministry. It is worth considering the resilience of some traditional reasons for the practice of evangelical poverty as recognized by several influential individuals, movements, spiritual developments, church documents, and other sources.

The Roman Catholic Vatican II Era and "Walking in the Way of Christ"

Various documents that emerged from the Second Vatican Council sought to aid Roman Catholic Christian disciples in their journey of maturing discipleship, rooted in their baptism and according to their particular call to live and give witness to the life and message of the gospel. Their common inspiration, the council stressed, should be from Jesus who lived

---

23. Thompson, *Bérulle and the French School*, 247–66.

and ministered "in poverty and persecution" as well as humility and self-sacrifice.[24] Christians are called to grow in expressing the self-giving love of Jesus in ways appropriate to their particular vocation of following Christ, whether in lay, consecrated, or ordained ministry; as part of this, they must be wary of inordinate attachments to wealth and possessions that can bind them to a world that is assuredly passing away.[25]

Men and women who live as consecrated religious profess the three evangelical counsels of celibate chastity, poverty, and obedience in the form of public vows, binding themselves more deeply to the celibate, poor, and obedient Christ. Their vowed practice of evangelical poverty is meant to be a reminder to all of the poor Christ who became poor so that all might become rich by his life and ministry. They should also take care to cultivate gospel poverty both in fact as well as in spirit, together with their religious brothers or sisters as part of a collective witness.[26] A subsequent document on consecrated life underscored the countercultural value that an authentically lived evangelical poverty could offer in the midst of a materialist culture, where individuals tend to measure self-worth in terms of possessions and can pay little heed to the exploitation and consumption of natural resources.[27]

The council also exhorted the practice of voluntary poverty among those who are called to ordained ministry but not members of consecrated religious institutes, so to more closely conform themselves to Christ in his attitudes of selflessness in ministry and his availability to persons of all economic classes.[28] Catholic priests are likewise counseled to do this as an aid to achieve Jesus' inner spiritual freedom, thereby rendering them more able to meet the demands of their vocation. This freedom requires a vibrant prayer life:

> On the subject of evangelical poverty, the synod fathers gave a concise yet important description, presenting it as "the subjection of all goods to the supreme good of God and his kingdom." In reality, only the person who contemplates and lives the mystery of God as the one and supreme good, as the true and definitive treasure, can understand and practice poverty, which is certainly not a matter of despising or rejecting material goods but of a loving

---

24. Paul VI, *Lumen Gentium*, no. 8.
25. Paul VI, *Lumen Gentium*, no. 42.
26. Paul VI, *Perfectae Caritatis*, no. 13.
27. John Paul II, *Vita Consecrata*, no. 89.
28. Paul VI, *Presbyterorum Ordinis*, no. 17.

and responsible use of these goods and at the same time an ability to renounce them with great interior freedom—that is, with reference to God and his plan.[29]

A Renewed Call to Solidarity with the Poor and Marginalized

In addition to several of the classic reasons for practicing evangelical poverty, another traditional one has reappeared beginning in the early twentieth century: that of fostering a stronger and more interdependent church as the body of Christ, through greater solidarity with the poor and marginalized of the world as a matter of social justice. Gospel poverty for the sake of greater community witness to Christ and the gospel continues to find support today in varying degrees across Christian denominations. The appeal to cultivating solidarity by way of voluntary poverty and simplicity has found energy from several notable sources.

Dorothy Day

An American, Day was a remarkable person who gave an inspiring witness to the counsel of voluntary poverty for much of the twentieth century. Responding to the plight of the economically poor and powerless workers, women, and those seeking world peace, Day followed a life of material austerity in her desire to identify with those she served. Together with Peter Maurin (1877–1949), she began the *Catholic Worker* in the early years of the Great Depression, a movement that continues today. The earlier years of her spirituality anticipated many principles of Christian life that would appear in Vatican II and later Roman Catholic documents.

Day's strong Christ-centered spirituality reflected her desire to follow the example of Jesus with all of her heart. A deeply prayerful woman despite her very active life, Day's Christian spirituality led her to appreciate Jesus who was to be found in all people but especially among the poor, homeless, and others on the margin of society. As Jesus did in his life, Day's practice of voluntary poverty was possible through her deep trust in God's loving providence to provide for both her needs and those of the *Catholic Worker* community. Her poverty also enabled her to be more present to

---

29. John Paul II, *Pastores Dabo Vobis*, no. 30.

the economically and socially marginalized, uniting in solidarity with those around her and with all of the world's poor.

Contemporary Roman Catholic Social Teaching

Echoing the fourth-century thought of Basil of Caesarea that recognized the responsibility of society to enable the development of all its members, Pope Paul VI (1897–1978) and later pontiffs have written that our intrinsic Christian solidarity with all persons includes those persons who are economically deprived. This commonality with the disadvantaged should sharpen our concern to alleviate whatever restrains them from a life of fundamental human dignity.

> Each man is also a member of society; hence he belongs to the community of man. It is not just certain individuals but all men who are called to further the development of human society as a whole. Civilizations spring up, flourish and die. As the waves of the sea gradually creep farther and farther in along the shoreline, so the human race inches its way forward through history.[30]

> We are the heirs of earlier generations, and we reap benefits from the efforts of our contemporaries; we are under obligation to all men. Therefore we cannot disregard the welfare of those who will come after us to increase the human family. The reality of human solidarity brings us not only benefits but also obligations.[31]

For the pope, the contemporary urgency is no less so than in the early Christian centuries. Surplus wealth of a society is meant to alleviate the suffering of those people left behind:

> We must repeat that the superfluous goods of wealthier nations ought to be placed at the disposal of poorer nations. The rule, by virtue of which in times past those nearest us were to be helped in time of need, applies today to all the needy throughout the world. And the prospering peoples will be the first to benefit from this. Continuing avarice on their part will arouse the judgment of God and the wrath of the poor, with consequences no one can foresee. If prosperous nations continue to be jealous of their own advantage alone, they will jeopardize their highest values, sacrificing the pursuit of excellence to the acquisition of possessions. We might

---

30. Paul VI, *Populorum Progressio*, no. 17.
31. Paul VI, *Populorum Progressio*, no. 17.

well apply to them the parable of the rich man. His fields yielded an abundant harvest and he did not know where to store it: "But God said to him, "Fool, this very night your soul will be demanded from you" (Luke 12:20).[32]

Liberation Theology and Spirituality

Liberation theology provides another source of Christian thought that has left a significant impact upon the awareness of both actual economic poverty and the spiritual practice of voluntary poverty. Originating in Latin America during the 1960s and owing much to the thought and writing of theologians such as Gustavo Gutierrez, modified expressions of liberation theology have taken root in most world regions. Its two principal poles are the historical Jesus, whose attitudes toward human beings and society are revealed through the Gospels, and the masses of economically poor individuals whose collective experience offers the setting for Christ to be found.

The poor of the Hebrew Testament—widows, orphans, laborers, outcasts—were God's favored ones; the Christian Scripture reveals that Jesus identified with the poor of his time as part of his freedom as a Son of God, announcing the presence of the reign of God and revealing the way for his disciples to follow as its inheritors. The practice of voluntary poverty is an essential dimension of identifying with the poor, enabling Christian disciples to be more readily available to them. The practice also assists in cultivating a sustained expression of solidarity as part of a "preferential option for the poor," thus assisting them to better see the world through their eyes and hopefully bring about a greater fullness of God's reign.

Ecological and Creation-Conscious Spiritualities

A fourth notable area of development has been from the growing appreciation for what is called "eco-spirituality" that flows from a respect for the gift of all creation and insight gained from the study of other spiritual traditions. To speak of an ecologically sensitive Christian spirituality is not new of course; it has long been very much at home within the Benedictine, Cistercian, Franciscan, and several other Christian religious traditions. However, the classic integrity between the spiritual and material realms of

---

32. Paul VI, *Populorum Progressio*, no. 49.

creation began to separate in the later medieval period, only gradually finding a recovery beginning in the nineteenth century.

An authentically Christian eco-spirituality is incarnational and recognizes that all of creation has the potential to express the majesty and the beauty of God's activity in the world. Creation may therefore be considered as *sacramental*, most notably so by virtue of Jesus' incarnation, and deserves reverence and respect as a divine gift and an instrument of God's ongoing creative activity. All of humanity is charged with the stewardship of creation and earth resources in a spirit of harmony toward creation and one another as cocreated daughters and sons of God, participants in the ongoing divine creativity. Another consequence of a Christian eco-spirituality is that creation and earth resources are meant to be used wisely by all persons rather than exploited for the profit of a few. This call for restraint in using world resources rather than profligacy is an unwelcome message for industrialist societies to accept, whose indifference can exacerbate such worldwide effects as environmental pollution, permanent scarring of the earth, the aggravation of global climate change, and other detriments.

Christian Poverty in Relationships with God, with Others, and as Part of Creation

The practice of evangelical or voluntary poverty has found a consistent place throughout the history of Christian spirituality, offering a variety of compelling reasons that continue to challenge contemporary disciples. A Christian spirituality influenced by some practice of evangelical poverty would touch not only the life of disciples, but also all of life around them.

With God

At the center for Christian disciples is the foundational desire to follow in the way of the historical Jesus. At least two reasons are apparent in this. One is his challenge to allow nothing to stand in the way of living ever more completely in the reign of God, as an excessive concern or grasping for material possessions tends to do. Second, while actual material poverty and the inability to meet basic human needs is hardly a blessing, Jesus' example nonetheless exhorts us to seek first the reign of God that includes confidence in God's love for us. That should be the one possession for which we aspire.

Voluntary Poverty for Greater Availability to the Spirit

Of course, this can seem in the present day as a wonderful but unattainable goal. Societies that are rooted in economic capitalism find their impetus to advance precisely through the consumption of goods, the more the better, offering a tempting though grotesque caricature of human life that glorifies material excess and an endless desire for something better than what one presently has. Meanwhile, Christian disciples who are content for many years with the same smart-phone and other modest engagements with capitalism can feel out of step with the rest of society. Also, what parents do not want the best for their child, not to mention the ability to provide for even basic needs such as clothing and health care? In truth, though, freedom from the excessive desire for material goods and the need to dwell in consumer competition for excessive and the latest possessions can give us a deeper freedom to live in the subtle yet real providential love of our Creator.

With Others

On the level of a Christian disciple's interpersonal relationships, some practice of evangelical poverty can be a way to express one's reverence and gratitude to God through giving to others in need. The wider Judeo-Christian prophetic tradition and several of the early church fathers particularly underscored that the poor find a special favor and sympathy with God. Christian disciples who grow in their love for God will tend to grow increasingly aware of what God loves and prefers. Contrary to what some Christians may believe, the call to solidarity through responding to the economic plight of our brothers and sisters worldwide, all children of our same Father, did not begin in the twentieth century.

As Part of Creation

At its broadest, encompassing the perspective of creation in which we all reside and of which we are part, voluntary poverty is a way to express one's personal stance in the world as gratefully accepting God's material gifts without needing to hoard them or make inordinate demands upon creation's natural resources. The practice of voluntary poverty finds a welcome home among many creation-centered Christians, considered necessary for one's ongoing growth in creation awareness. A lasting transformation of world consciousness and harmonization with all creation must begin with growth of individual awareness of the issue through a deliberate, habitual, and prayer-rooted openness to the divine source of all life. Voluntary poverty brings one's personal existence into a more authentic lived reality that pushes back against the forces of consumerism and its devouring of natural resources due to unbridled excess and uncritical spending, opting for an attitude that chooses sustainability over profligacy. It also keeps one mindful of those throughout the world who suffer due to the imbalance of wealth and exploitation of resources, promoting an attitude of solidarity with them.

In conclusion, cultivating the virtue of evangelical poverty has potentially wide-reaching effect for the life of a Christian disciple. To the degree that we are able to practice it, voluntary poverty sets us at the disposition of the Holy Spirit who guides and moves within us. Voluntary poverty challenges us to be willing participants in the Spirit's renewal of humanity and the world; it moves us to living in solidarity with our brothers and sisters who are less blessed than ourselves; and it helps us to share with others more respectfully the blessings of creation that are present in its myriad resources. Evangelical poverty can thus assist in fashioning our lives into an expression of thanksgiving to our Creator, to whom we are indebted for all that we hold and may acquire.

6

Fortitude for Steadfast Christian Discipleship

FORTITUDE ADDRESSES OUR ACTIONS and reactions in the face of danger and fear. The multifaceted virtue of fortitude is frequently translated into English as courage but is much more. Courage may commonly be understood as the response to situations calling for bravery and overlooking one's personal safety, while fortitude is classically understood as a more-encompassing virtue, enabling a person to endure hardship, physical suffering, and even death for the sake of something that is loved more than oneself. Besides governing the exercise of one's personal courage between extremes of cowardice and recklessness, fortitude also helps to guide one's appropriate response to a given hardship or threat. There are times when one must actively resist and struggle against a situation with all of one's might, while other situations may call for the person's patient acceptance and endurance of the difficulty.

From ancient Greek times, fortitude has been considered as one of the primary (or *cardinal*) moral virtues to develop in order for persons to achieve their true happiness, by maintaining their personal integrity in following their deepest convictions.[1] Since, for Christians, God should be our greatest good, Christian fortitude strengthens them to live according to Christian beliefs in the face of suffering and even death.

The virtue of fortitude receives less written attention among classical Christian writers as have the others in this book such as poverty, chastity,

---

1. The other cardinal virtues are prudence, justice, and temperance.

and the like, perhaps because fortitude was regarded as one of the four primary virtues of Greek classical thought and was only gradually accepted as an appropriate Christian quality. Nonetheless, testimony to the presence of fortitude frequently shines forth throughout the Judeo-Christian tradition, and Christian history holds many occasions where a Christ-inspired fortitude appears in the lives of especially heroic figures. However, the presence of fortitude frequently needs to be "teased out" from individual lives through a broader historical analysis, providing inspirational examples throughout the centuries.

I. CHRISTIAN FORTITUDE THROUGH THE CENTURIES

Fortitude in the Scriptures

The Old Testament

The Hebrew Scripture does not specifically mention fortitude, but gives plentiful evidence of persistent courage. The people of God valued courage as a necessary warrior quality, fruit of their faithfulness and obedience to God, during their long and frequently battle-scarred pilgrimage from the time of Abraham. Elsewhere, one often finds the admonition given to "take courage!" as when David exhorted the rebuilders of the temple to "be strong and of good courage" for the immense task ahead (1 Chr 22:3), and to his son Solomon to "be strong and of good courage, and act" to begin constructing the Ark of the Covenant (1 Chr 28:20).

God's people could hope to be courage-filled so long as they were faithful to God and recognized that it was God who strengthened their hearts and arms for battle, as did David before his victory over Goliath (1 Sam 17:37). Personal and social failure in obedience, however, threatened the loss of their precious store; for example, when God chastised Ezekiel's listeners for their unfaithfulness:

> See, I strike my hands together at the dishonest gain you have made, and at the blood that has been shed within you. Can your courage endure, or can your hands remain strong in the days when I shall deal with you? I the Lord have spoken, and I will do it. I will scatter you among the nations and disperse you through the countries, and I will purge your filthiness out of you.[2]

---

2. Ezek 22:13–15.

While the people exhorted one another to courage in the face of overwhelming difficulty and in military campaigns, there were also calls to a deeper persevering courage to confront the numerous assailants who persecuted the faithful of Israel. The Maccabean literature recounts such moments, as when the elder Eleazar accepted a ferocious death by being broken on a wheel for refusing to eat of meat sacrificed to idols, "as all ought to go who have the courage to refuse things that it is not right to taste, even for the natural love of life" (2 Macc 6:20). A mother and her seven sons each went to their death by dismemberment and other abuses; each son was strengthened by the words of his mother who found within herself a great resolute, persevering, and patient courage as she watched them go, one by one, to their death. The author exhorted listeners that the mother should be especially honored for her courage and faith in her God during the ordeal, considered during his time to be masculine qualities, recounting that "filled with a noble spirit, she reinforced her woman's reasoning with a man's courage" (2 Macc 7:20).

The New Testament

Jesus as portrayed in the Gospels offers ample evidence of the place of fortitude. His life of deepest communion and unity of love with his heavenly father afforded Jesus a truly sustaining life in the Holy Spirit through whom issues all virtue and spiritual gifts. His willingness to proclaim the *kerygma* and criticize the Jewish leaders on several occasions, the moment he set his face to go to Jerusalem (Luke 9:51) and accepted the dangers of entering there for the dramatic climax, his passive acceptance of his brutal suffering and the rejection by his people that were wrought by his passion and crucifixion, all reveal Jesus' courage that was more than simple bravery. It was, rather, courage sustained in perseverance and patience that fortitude brought to bear in his life and ministry.

The fortitude of his mother Mary, noted especially in the Lukan Gospel, gives further witness to the place of this virtue in the life of those who live in fidelity and obedience to God. Luke's representations of Mary reveal several moments when she was challenged to accept the mysterious ways that God was working through her life. The visit by the angel (1:26–38), announcing that she was to become the mother of the son of God through the action of the Holy Spirit and outside the normal way of marriage, would also have brought the risks of social shame and perhaps even death for having dishonored her betrothed spouse. Her willingness to journey with Joseph to Bethlehem on donkey-back toward the end of her pregnancy in order to fulfill the census requirement carried numerous hazards for her due to her vulnerable state of health (2:1–6). Different moments of Jesus' ministerial life would have been difficult for her, especially as his ministry increasingly placed him in conflict with the Jewish religious establishment and his people. In all of these, it is not difficult to perceive the activity of fortitude in the life of this faithful, exemplary daughter of Israel, at once mother and trusting disciple of Jesus.

The early years of the post-resurrection followers and proclaimers of the good news reveal some of the difficulties that Jesus' early apostles had to face with resolute and, no doubt, at times imperfect courage. Followers of the new movement known as "the Way" initially considered themselves as a sect within Judaism. While the Jews were no strangers to such movements, there were occasions where the two groups would clash; at times the Christian disciples would suffer bodily injury or even death for proclaiming Jesus as the fulfilment of the Old Testament, as did the deacon Stephen who accepted his stoning while beholding a heavenly vision of Jesus at God's right hand (Acts 7). The apostle Paul was a man filled with the Holy Spirit who encouraged and strengthened him throughout his four mission journeys throughout the Mediterranean world, leading to his death at the hands of the Roman Empire. Peter, too, traditionally considered at first as an impulsive and not very courageous man, was head of the Jerusalem church along with James "the just"; both of them risked danger and endured hardship over the course of some thirty years and were ultimately killed in service to proclaiming the gospel message. Each of these cases required the courage and perseverance found in the virtue of fortitude.

This brief foray into the scriptural portrayals of courage and fortitude reveals diverse applications of fortitude. Whether during the Old Testament times of battle, the inter-testament Maccabean period, or along the historical arc of the New Testament, one finds many calls for the strength and endurance that the virtue provides. The early Christian church was struggling to exist in the midst of different intensities of persecution and martyrdom, a condition that would persist from the middle first until the early fourth centuries. Martyrdom came to typify for Christian disciples the summit of holiness; whether in the actual suffering of persecution and martyrdom that is found even in the present day, or the bloodless though formative calls to personal faithfulness through which God's ineffable plan would be realized. Both of these experiences required the presence and practice of fortitude, albeit in differing degrees.

Fortitude in the Patristic Era

The Church Fathers

As the early Christian communities gradually formed their own identity due in part to their separation from their Jewish roots, they also became increasingly vulnerable to derision and attack from both Jewish adherents and the surrounding pagan religions of the Greco-Roman empire. Early Christian literature is rich with exhortations from notable church leaders to the Christian communities, seeking to strengthen their adherence to their Christian faith that found itself challenged on two fronts. One was maintaining their Christian identity and communion with one another despite the numerous challenges from heterodox Christian movements that appeared in parts of the Christian world; the other was to withstand the relentless array of corruptive influences from their pagan societies with which they interacted daily. Church leaders also needed to be reassured in their duty as shepherds in protecting their flocks, as Ignatius of Antioch wrote in support of his fellow-bishop Polycarp of Smyrna:

> Let not those who seem worthy of credit, but teach strange doctrines fill you with apprehension. Stand firm, as does an anvil which is beaten. It is the part of a noble athlete to be wounded, and yet to conquer. And especially, we ought to bear all things for the sake of God, that He also may bear with us. Be ever becoming more zealous than what you are. Weigh carefully the times. Look for Him who is above all time, eternal and invisible, yet who became visible for our sakes; impalpable and impassible, yet who became passable on our account; and who in every kind of way suffered for our sakes.[3]

The image of an athlete recurs in Ignatius's exhortations to readiness for whenever moments of trial would surely arise. Indeed, Ignatius was on his way to Rome to face martyrdom following his fearless confrontation with the Emperor Trajan; his own words express some of the self-denial that his fortitude required. For example, Ignatius pleaded with the Roman

---

3. Ign. *Pol.* 3.

Christian community not to allow sentimentality to obscure his impending death, hoping to be a worthy disciple of Christ:

> Surely I do not want you to court the good pleasure of men, but to please God, as indeed you do please him . . . For, if you quietly ignore me, I am the word of God; but if you fall in love with my human nature, I shall, on the contrary, be a mere sound. Grant me no more than that you let my blood be spilled in sacrifice to God . . . How glorious to be a setting sun—away from the world, on to God![4]

Ignatius also implored the prayers of the community for persevering courage as he longed to meet his death as a faithful Christian and not as one who would fail in the face of suffering, asking disciples to "Only beg for me strength within and without, that I may be a man not merely of words, but also of resolution. In this way I shall not only be called a Christian, but also prove to be one."[5]

The intermittent periods of persecution were initially local in nature through the early third century with the emergence of increasingly vicious pursuits of Christians, often for their refusal to participate in Roman pagan religious and imperial worship. From the first century, both women and men resolutely met their violent death rather than compromising their core beliefs in the one true God. The collection of martyrdom accounts that have entered the Christian tradition, while perhaps embellishing at times the objective circumstances of their deaths, illustrate the reverence with which the Christian community honored and extolled the fortitude of these spiritual athletes. For example, *The Martyrdom of Perpetua and Felicitas* (written ca. 202) recounts the ordeal and death in Carthage of at least five baptismal catechumens; among them was Perpetua, a young woman of good upbringing with an infant at the breast, and her servant Felicitas. The group welcomed baptism despite the sufferings inflicted on Christians of her time and were condemned to various forms of gruesome death in the arena. A segment of Perpetua's ordeal is believed to be from her personal account, revealing the extent to which her fortitude was tested even before entering the amphitheater. It includes having to endure extended periods of time together with her child in the fetid, dark, and dank confines of the communal dungeon, the earnest pleadings of her father to concede to the demands of the officials, and her maternal fear for her child that she ultimately relinquished into the care of others. Accounts such as these served

---

4. Ign. *Rom.* 2.
5. Ign. *Rom.* 3.

to strengthen the faith and fortitude of other Christians for whom such suffering was a real threat.

Tertullian, a contemporary of Perpetua and Felicity, addressed a question that may seem peculiar for contemporary readers; the issue of whether Christians should flee from persecution and its dangers or, rather, meet it head-on in a confrontation with their society and authorities. His response was that they should hold fast and face the danger, for several reasons. One was that God was Lord over all created things and situations; thus moments of persecution were under the divine gaze and, in effect, part of the divine will for all of God's people. Also, we should not try to escape from our moment of suffering because no one can truly evade what God intends for the person; the time had arrived for the Christian to profess his or her faith, love, and trust in God alone who always accompanies us through every trial, remembering that only God is deserving of our fear.[6] Alas, not all Christians would be able to stand up to their tormentors; still, Tertullian noted of their possible suffering and resolute persistence that "the one great thing in persecution is the promotion of the glory of God, as He tries and casts away, lays on and takes off."[7]

One must remember that Tertullian and most of the earlier church elders were remarkably zealous Christian disciples who shared a view that the authentic path of Christianity demanded great personal asceticism in confronting the surrounding pagan world. While Tertullian's attitude may repel us, he did raise at least one good point for discipleship even beyond the likelihood of persecution and death. Namely, that a profession of faith carries more weight when one suffers some inconvenience or loss because of it, revealing the "pearl of great price" that one has discovered and will not easily relinquish.

The Post-Nicene Period

The cessation of systematic Christian persecutions with the 313 Edict of Milan, followed by the empire-wide normalization of the Christian religion, provided a much easier path for early Christian discipleship. At the same time, it exacted a cost. While Christians could live almost entirely without fear of suffering for their faith, it also contributed to a moral and spiritual laxity in following the Christian life and a greater openness to the

---

6. Tertullian, *Fug.* 9.
7. Tertullian, *Fug.* 1.

corrupting influences of the surrounding non-Christian cultures. Many Christians, whose fortitude and other virtues had been ascetically tempered during the years of suffering and danger, began to seek more disciplined paths of Christian life that would help to strengthen their interior mettle. From the time of the apostle Paul, many Christians wishing to devote themselves entirely to following the way of Jesus would typically adopt a life of virginity. This practice, combined with a fourth-century desire among many Christians to put distance between themselves and what they regarded as a compromised society and church community, contributed to the development of early eremitic or solitary Christian monastic life in the wilderness. There they were challenged to practice their fortitude in observing a lifelong daily round of prayer, enduring the relentless heat of the desert sun and the ache of loneliness, while otherwise struggling against temptations to abandon their ascetical proving ground.[8] Continuing into the present day, both solitary and cenobitic (communal) varieties of Christian monasticism place a high regard for the rigors and hardships accepted in their yearning to be closer to Christ.

Bishop Ambrose of Milan (339–97) gave considerable attention to the needs of a bishop as shepherd of a large Christian community. One serving in this office should steadfastly cling to the apostolic Church tradition and not be deterred by such concerns as personal respect (fear of losing the good opinion of others) or losing the peaceful support of his people. The first book of Ambrose's series *On the duties of the clergy* reveals his familiarity with the four cardinal virtues that he deemed as essential for a bishop to cultivate to fulfill his ministry of spiritual and moral guidance. For Ambrose, Christian fortitude was necessary in order to cultivate and keep the other virtues; it also strengthened a bishop to preach the truth of the gospel without succumbing to the fear of losing the good opinion or favor of others.[9]

We find at the close of the patristic centuries that fortitude was already a prized quality for Christian disciples, tempered by the first centuries of persecution and martyrdom, recognized as an important component for Christian life and ministry.

---

8. Eremitic monasticism was already known before the fourth century, as attested by the story of Antony of Egypt of the later third-century and other monks who fled the world and its temptations; the fourth-century situation of Christian life evidently fueled the popularity of this lifestyle.

9. Ambrose, *Off.* 1.25.119.

Fortitude in the Medieval Era

Early-Medieval Period

Early Western medieval monasticism offers examples of fortitude while Christianity was stretching beyond the civilized environs of Europe into the most remote and uncivilized regions, following the collapse of the Roman Empire. The resulting spread of monasticism offered a missionary fruitfulness, as well as its dangers, calling forth the virtue of fortitude from its monks. In some cases, Celtic monks such as Columban (543–615) would embrace the penitential practice of exile as pilgrims (*peregrini*) and leave their first community in hope of establishing another foundation in remote parts of Europe or elsewhere, in all likelihood never returning to their homeland, while fortified by the characteristic rigors of their monastic vocation.[10] Another monk, Augustine of Canterbury (d. 604), was sent by Pope Gregory the Great, along with a small group of confreres, from Rome to the southwest of Britain with the mission of establishing the Christian faith among the subjects of the pagan King Ethelbert. During their journey from Rome by sea to southern Gaul, then traveling through the Frankish territories and across the North Sea to Kent, the band of forty-odd members suffered disunity among themselves and begged Augustine to reconsider his papal mission. Augustine returned to Rome to confer with the pope, whereupon Gregory ordered him to recommit himself to his brothers and their noble pursuit. Their persistence resulted in a Christian missionary foothold in southern Britain and the foundation of the great Benedictine monastery and church presence at Canterbury.[11] The fortitude of many such monastics helped to spread Christianity ever further beyond the then-known world.

High- and Later-Medieval Periods

The life of the martyr Thomas Becket (1118–70) serves to illustrate his apparent exercise of fortitude in the sometimes-uneasy relationship that existed between church spiritual authority and the civil rule of royalty, or between the two spheres of cross and crown. On the European continent, the rising hegemony of the emperor Frederick I had begun casting its

---

10. Smither, *Missionary Monks*, 81.
11. Smither, *Missionary Monks*, 85–87.

shadow over the Italian peninsula and posed a threat to the independence of the Roman church. Bishops and cardinals were compelled to align either on the side of Pope Alexander III who sought to maintain the freedom of the Western Christian church, or with the anti-pope Victor IV who supported the more invasive imperial policies.[12]

In England, King Henry II desired to regain a greater degree of influence in ecclesiastical affairs that his father had once enjoyed as king. Becket, Henry's longtime friend, was serving as a capable court chancellor when Henry appointed him in 1162 as archbishop of Canterbury, a key position through which the king hoped to control the church in England. Before his installation, Becket was a faithful attendant to the king while always vigilant toward protecting the integrity of the church in the spirit of Alexander III. Becket had earnestly sought to avoid the appointment, foreseeing the inevitable clash with Henry; once installed, the new archbishop adopted a humble life of penance and study in seeking to honor and fulfill the seriousness of his new vocation and to protect the rights of the Christian church in the face of mounting pressure to collaborate. The first serious incident occurred when Henry sought to extend royal jurisdiction over church clergy accused of crimes, followed by an attempt to reassert royal approval for episcopal appointments and demand their oath of fealty to the crown. Becket stood practically alone among the other bishops in his refusal, which led to his enduring a six-year exile to France under the protection of Louis VII. Ultimately agreeing to return to Canterbury amid royal promises of returned lands and respect for church freedoms, Becket again was forced to stand against royal pressure to support the lift of an earlier excommunication that had been placed on several royal councilors.

Becket's 1170 murder in the cathedral by four knights was apparently the result of a misunderstood wish uttered by the king; still, Becket continued to show his persevering courage at the moment of his death. When he refused the knights' order upon threat of death to rescind the excommunications, Becket is reported to have said that he was willing to die for the sake of God and the church if peace and liberty would thus be restored.[13] Clearly, the last several years of Thomas Becket's life had demanded of him a long practice of the courage and perseverance of fortitude for the sake of his beliefs and sense of duty, surely one reason for the special place he has held among the martyred heroes of the Western Christian church.

12. Jedin and Dolan, *History of the Church*, 4:51–56.
13. Jedin and Dolan, *History of the Church*, 4:72.

Fortitude for Steadfast Christian Discipleship

Confronting established powerful organizations and challenging their misuse of power, whether civil or religious, is never easy; the long arc of western history holds many reminders of the steep cost for some reform-minded individuals. The Christian church of the high and later medieval period bore many signs of internal corruption among its clergy and different levels of leadership, including within the papal court. The conditions of the time sparked numerous reform movements such as among the twelfth-century Waldensians, initially desiring a return to the Gospel ideals of Jesus and the simplicity of the primitive Christian church. Lay-founded itinerant groups wandered the thirteenth-century European countryside preaching the need for church reform and a higher standard of moral life; others, such as the Beghards and Beguines, pursued their ideal in stable communities. While one may dispute the later religious viewpoint of some movements that were ultimately judged by church authority as heretical or by the civil arm as seditious, we cannot but admire their fortitude in pursuing their convictions that brought many of them prolonged personal hardship, physical torture, and even death.

Scholastic theologians of the high medieval period such as Thomas Aquinas also struggled with the virtue of fortitude, though within the safer realms of academia and theology.[14] Aquinas recognized fortitude as one of the four great virtues from ancient Greek thought, indeed as a cardinal ("hinge") virtue since other virtues are affected by it. Fortitude as a virtue allows a Christian disciple to overcome fear and so endure in struggling against some evil, the greatest human evil being the threat of losing one's life or something else that is cherished; the greatest Christian fear would be to offend God and lose eternal salvation. Two elements are in play here that draw on fortitude; resist and attack. The principal concern is to strengthen one's endurance in resisting some evil, the more difficult of the two. The principal word here is *endurance*, while also calling on four "lesser" or subservient qualities that comprise parts of fortitude. The other element is the need to thoughtfully regulate one's measured response in attacking or otherwise responding to vanquish the evil. Besides the virtues of courage, patience, and perseverance that are contained within fortitude, one is also challenged to exercise other subservient qualities or "parts" of the virtue, namely, an effective quality of *magnanimity* (to be a person of "great mind" or "great spirit" who can imagine and desire to achieve great things) and

---

14. *Summa* II-II, q. 123.

magnificence (the ability to make sacrifices and overcome obstacles to doing great things that are suggested by one's magnanimity).

Just as all moral virtues are best exercised in moderation between two possible extremes, so fortitude seeks to regulate our human effort to overcome some evil by doing good between those of cowardice (or timidity) and foolhardiness (or reckless daring).

Fortitude in the Modern Era

The English Christian Persecutions

The onset of the Protestant Reformation spawned many opportunities for devout Christians, Roman Catholic or not, to follow their religious convictions through travails of rejection, suffering, and death. In the English-speaking world, perhaps the most-documented period has included the successive waves of persecutions in England during the sixteenth- and seventeenth-century reigns of Henry VIII (1509–47), Mary I "Queen of Scots" (1553–58), and Elizabeth I (1558–1603).

Henry's rule evolved from his papal recognition as "Defender of the Faith" for his apologetic writing in support of the Catholic sacraments against Lutheran criticism, to that of cleaving from Rome to initiate the Church of England. Anxious to produce a male successor to his throne, he had failed to acquire a Roman annulment of his marriage to Catherine of Aragon in order to marry Anne Boleyn. Henry soon thereafter demanded that all subjects and clergy recite his oath of succession upon pain of imprisonment and death, which would secure their recognition of Anne as queen.

Sir Thomas More (1478–1535) was one of the few individuals who would not acquiesce to the king. A married layman and firmly committed Roman Catholic with a distinguished legal career, More had been a confidant of the king for many years and served professionally at Henry's court for three of them. Gradually, though, More's misgivings increased as Henry pressed his desire for the annulment. In the end, More could not support the dissolution of a valid and binding Catholic marriage. He resigned from his chancellorship position into retirement as the controversy grew, ostensibly for health reasons. However, he was once again forced to confront the issue when demanded to accept the Act of Supremacy that effectively recognized the king as head of the church in England. More refused, holding to his belief that the Roman church alone was the guarantor of salvation, and was committed to the Tower of London.

Henry sought a marriage endorsement from the influential More, hoping for more than a year that More would acquiesce. More had to repeatedly defend his position before the king's representatives while initially enjoying such privileges as reading and writing materials and visits from his wife and adult children. These were gradually withdrawn, as well as family visiting privileges, and family relations became increasingly strained since Thomas would never reveal the reasons for his position. Henry's patience was finally exhausted. In July 1535, More was judged guilty of treason (in effect having denied the king's lawful place as ruler of the church in England) and initially left to expect a treasoner's horrible death by evisceration and dismemberment (to be "drawn, hanged, and quartered"), though in fact he was more mercifully beheaded five days later. According to later newspaper accounts, More's final words proclaimed that he was dying "in the faith and for the faith of the Catholic Church, the king's good servant, but God's first."[15]

Henry's daughter Mary assumed the throne upon the king's death, restoring Roman Catholicism for a time as the religion of the realm while suppressing the reform. Close to three hundred Anglican reformers were killed during her reign as "Bloody Mary." Protestant resistance grew and the deposed Mary was herself beheaded on the order of her sister Elizabeth, who once again suppressed Catholic Masses and other Roman religious practice upon threat of death for treason. This was a time of hushed Roman Catholic Masses among small groups of trusted faithful that were furtively celebrated in their homes, and of "priest holes" where a cleric would hope to hide undetected, sometimes for days, in the event of a surprise raid by authorities. English priests such as the Jesuit Edmund Campion left their homeland to attended seminary in Catholic France and returned to endure a secretive, dangerous, and often short-lived ministry in their homeland (Campion was drawn, hanged, and quartered for treason in 1581 at the infamous scaffold known as the "Tyburn Tree").

These are only some of the examples of Christian fortitude that emerged during the sixteenth-century period of English Christian persecution from Christian disciples of different denominations.

---

15. As reported in the *Paris News Letter* account of the execution; Reynolds, *Trial of Saint Thomas More*, 151. Reynolds noted elsewhere in the book that, while the *News Letter* was a reasonably trustworthy account, other execution reports differed somewhat.

Christian Missionaries

Lived fortitude was also apparent in the Christian missionary efforts to other parts of the world beginning in the sixteenth century, calling for courage, patience, and endurance of suffering in defense or support of the Christian faith in the midst of hardship and threat of death. Roman Catholic congregations such as the Jesuits, Franciscans, and Dominicans were eventually followed by other congregations of both men and women from both Catholic and other Christian denominations who would leave their familiar homeland to assist in establishing and sustaining the Christian faith in remote regions. Their members frequently endured deprivations, isolation, sometimes repeated episodes of torture and sickness for the sake of proclaiming and witnessing to the gospel in foreign lands, far away from their home that many would never see again.

On the eve of the twentieth century, we find that the virtue of fortitude has been a fruitful if not a sublime component of Christian life. Whether in the lives of persecuted Christians, missionaries, or those of high office, their courage was thankfully strengthened by the grace to discern what they truly cherished in terms of human striving and even human life itself. The perseverance and patience offered by fortitude allowed them to bear and confront the burden of their fears and uncertainties over extended periods of time.

II. TOWARD A CONTEMPORARY APPRECIATION FOR CHRISTIAN FORTITUDE

The need for fortitude still arises in our present-day world, though most of us may prefer to admire and honor its presence vicariously, in the lives of others.

As noted earlier, the virtue of fortitude is broader than the simple exercise of courage; it also helps to guide our emotional responses to confront our particular challenge. One may speak of the exercise of courage in many ways. *Physical* courage is that which is needed for feats of physical bravery, also known as valor experienced in battle or other situations requiring the risking of one's life to save another. *Moral* courage is when one is compelled to act or otherwise hold to their deeply-held beliefs in the presence of social pressure, rejection of family or other close acquaintances. The Christian spiritual tradition also offers examples of what may be called *mystical* courage in the pursuit of spiritual growth and maturity, maintaining a life of prayer in the face of perceived alienation by God as they traveled their mysterious and ineffable spiritual journey.[16] Whether for physical, moral, or spiritual reasons, fortitude continues to be in demand today.

To appreciate the need for Christian fortitude, recall that the virtue helps to overcome the effect of fear by keeping one's response to fear between the two extremes of cowardice and recklessness. The word cowardice fosters a strong negative connotation; wartime novels such as the English classic *The Four Feathers* (Mason, 1902) and *The Execution of Private Slovik* (Huie, 1954) both illustrated the social abhorrence for nineteenth—and twentieth-century wartime cowardice. Most people will never find their courage tested by the fear encountered in life-or-death battle conditions; however, what about more ordinary experiences of *timidity*? Timidity is found among many individuals, for a host of reasons; while not as visceral a word as cowardice, timidity can also limit the quality of life for someone due to the presence of a particular fear.

Recklessness is also a word that conjures certain images, usually associated with excessive acts of bravery; teenagers testing their self-confidence in front of one other as they stand on the ledge of a high-rise building or a rocky cliff; a motorcycle jumper who soars over a line of cars or other objects; an exuberant parachutist who delays pulling his or her ripcord in order to enjoy a few more seconds of perilous free-fall. Many if not most people might tend to shy away from such exhibitions of daring (advancing age has a way of bringing that!). But there are other less-recognized types of recklessness that can be dangerous. One case would be religious recklessness in casually believing that God will ultimately see one through a risky venture involving financial investment or another poorly considered project in the name of some good cause. Another, medical recklessness, could include the repeated pushing of one's physical health past the level of exhaustion for some personal greater good, risking physical health or even mental balance. While the particular cherished "greater goods" are not to be easily discounted, nor should traditional examples of God's faithfulness to God's people, such types of recklessness do exist in contemporary life and must be somehow evaluated and governed in responding to the situation.

Besides helping to sustain one's courageous response, fortitude also seeks to guide the degree of one's active reaction against it. The threat to

---

16. Two such mystics were Teresa of Avila (1515–82) and Mother Teresa of Calcutta (1910–97), as related through some of their spiritual works.

one's life or other cherished possession normally incites the desire to *do* something, whether to kill the adversary in self-defense, to destroy the reputation of another as a response to their verbal attacks; or contrarily, whether to passively permit and endure the abuses as a gospel-inspired strategy. This latter response was the way of Jesus in accepting his unjust Passion and death; it also has been embraced as a deliberate response of non-violence in the face of aggression and violent threats, such as that of Martin Luther King Jr. and countless other people who have stood up against injustice. Such passive response in the face of evil is actually more difficult than activity, requiring more endurance, patience, and even faith, and is more dependent on the virtue of fortitude. Different life situations calling for Christian fortitude will demand different degrees of active or passive responses to the threat according to the circumstances, requiring an attitude of discernment in light of Jesus and the gospel.

The past century has revealed many moments in which individuals have chosen to embrace their deeply-held beliefs in the face of physical and moral adversity, revealing that fortitude can well up from both Christian and non-Christian sources. Dorothy Day was jailed several times in the United States for her relentless pursuit of social justice issues, first as a political revolutionary, later for following her radical interpretation of the Christian gospel. Many Christians have persevered in following the gospel while being threatened and often killed due to twenty-first-century hatred of their faith in Egypt and other countries of the Middle East and Africa.

The elements of fortitude can also arise from deeply-held patriotism alongside Christian beliefs. One example is that of the pastor Dietrich Bonhoeffer, imprisoned and finally killed for his religious stand against Jewish extermination and the cultural spread of Nazism. Another would be former naval aviator and senator John McCain (1936–2018) who, though able to leave, chose to remain with his fellow American prisoners in a squalid enemy military prison and endured several more years of torture and pain. Other individuals have shown an undeniable fortitude as members of non-Christian faith traditions, as in the life and death of Mahatma Gandhi who, between 1903 and his murder in 1947, sought a greater social justice for Indian people in both Transvaal (present-day South Africa) and in his native India. These people are among the first that come to mind when considering contemporary demands for the courage, perseverance, and patience found in the virtue of fortitude.

In our present day, fortitude becomes an important though perhaps underrated quality in lives that are not so unusual. The married couple who agree to remain together for the sake of their children rather than abandoning an apparently lifeless marriage (assuming there is no physical danger to anyone in the family, of course); the government civil servant who risks job and career by having to stand up as a whistleblower while enduring rejection and the threat of financial repercussion; individuals across the globe who promote lifestyle practices respecting the environment in the face of large-money interests that become increasingly hostile to their message; for these and many other people, ethically-guided fortitude is an essential quality. The specifically Christian practice of fortitude will be founded, of course, by following the moral example of Jesus who sought to be faithful to the Father's call that he perceived, trusting that the Father's love for him would strengthen and never abandon him.

Christian Fortitude in Relationships with God, with Others, and as Part of Creation

With God

Personal fear can inhibit our relationship with God in Christ. So many people live fearful lives that impede a fuller discipleship, victims of timidity and even cowardice. The manifestations and reasons are many. Some personal fears can be deeply rooted, resulting from developmental issues such as a lack of security during childhood, perhaps resulting from an unstable or irregular family structure. Others suffer fear caused by some past disappointment; a fear of intimacy that keeps them from the blessings of deep relationships, failure in some professional or financial endeavor, or perhaps simply the fear of an uncertain future that effectively shackles a person to some predictable yet stultifying routine of life. Also, individuals can suffer from inordinate cynicism and have lost the ability to trust in the structures of church and society. The scars from these fears are real, part of the cost of life in a wounded human nature and a largely uncontrollable creation. Although past personal wounds and scars may not be totally restricting and God's love can work in us despite them, an attitude of timidity to live more fully that results from our fears can effectively keep us from more actively engaging in life and participating in our Christian vocation and discipleship. Each of these, to at least some degree, betrays a lack of confidence in the divine hand that holds all of our deepest hopes, aspirations, and dreams, that created us and continues to unfurl us into the unique disciple that each of us represents. Each will challenge us to develop a mature and healthy confidence in God who accompanies us at every moment in life.

Confidence in God is a concrete expression of the virtue of hope, one of the three "supernatural" virtues as taught in Roman Catholic theology along with those of faith and charity.[17] While growth in faith helps us to accept an ever-expanding perception of who God is and how God acts, the virtue of hope strengthens our ability to accept that God can and does indeed continue to reveal God's self to us as we navigate through the challenges, joys, and failures of our lives and so deepen our faith in God. Personal fears that have wormed their way into our lives and cause our habitual timid response to life challenges can limit our ability to accept the potential of divine activity that we cannot measure, an important element from which fortitude can draw strength.

Historical examples of many Christian martyrs and other spiritual heroes reveal the potential for the virtue of fortitude when there is present a confident hope toward God, helping to form a firm base from which to face the many challenges of life and faith with an attitude of trust in the divine providence permeating all of creation.

With Others

Contemporary human society provides endless challenges calling for Christian fortitude. Human scientific and social progress march ahead while a sufficient Christian-based ethic to guide them may not be sufficiently developed to adequately address the moral challenges that can result. Nevertheless, the Spirit foments personal or communal Christian witnesses against such evils as abortion, euthanasia, and unethical reasons behind genetic manipulation. Christian discipleship depends on fortitude in the seemingly endless confrontations with such evils and their corresponding call to resist them. This is especially true for disciples who take an active and extended participation, such as groups who maintain a weekly or even daily prayer vigil in front of abortion clinics, week after week, month after month, often

---

17. The other two supernatural virtues are faith (in which we mature spiritually through broadening our ability to accept who God is and how God is active). The other is charity or love (the capacity for being able to love others with the totally self-giving, other-absorbed love that describes the interrelationship of the Father, Son, and Holy Spirit).

while having to endure name-calling, insults, and sometimes even violent opposition. Their courage, patience, perseverance, and measured response to the evil all indicate the active presence of Christian fortitude.

The unity of Christian family life is sorely tried by the stresses and mores in much of contemporary society and suffers much the same as what is endured by non-Christians. One's Christian faith is but one essential ingredient; the other is the witness provided by witnessing before others to the presence of Christ in all places, before all evil, and that the love of God will eventually triumph over all evil. While this is a basic element of Christian belief, it calls for great endurance, patience, and Spirit-guided courage.

As Part of Creation

Our fears can influence important life decisions such as choosing a life career direction. Refusal to acknowledge the presence of one's fear of relationships or personal encounters can unfortunately drive one into a career path that has a minimum of interpersonal contact. Fear of personal failure can cause one to choose a less risky career direction that is void of the passion and fulfillment that is found when one's personal talents and interest are better engaged. Short-sighted choices made because of fear thus would have an effect on one's participation in the ongoing order of creation and divine activity in the overall arena of social and individual human progress.

Such weighty human decisions require a certain courage to experiment with possibilities, to formulate a plan, and to muster the perseverance to bring the choice to fruition. Years of study, scraping together the needed finances, perhaps alongside the primary requirements of marriage and family, all of these should rightly give pause when making a personal decision that would impact so many others. Fortitude is essential in order to support one's plan to achieve the elected goal, hoping for a more life-giving participation in the ongoing process of creation that is meant to follow the Creator's ongoing design for it.

Fortitude also can serve the neverending efforts to offer better stewardship of creation. Some individuals will do so in a more visible prophetic way, such as the followers of Sr. Dorothy Stang in her stance against industrial exploitation of the Amazon forest. Other Christians persistently offer a Christian voice of conscience in seeking to care for our common creation in service to the well-being of the environment.

From Strength to Strength

The virtue of fortitude has been an important quality for Christian disciples since the time of Jesus. Fortitude has helped make possible the expansion of the Christian church and has supported Christian witness to the truth of the Christian message. Practicing fortitude not only elicits courage in confronting the threat to someone or something cherished, it also helps us to endure even suffering and death for the sake of our fidelity to the gospel. There should be no doubt that Christian fortitude will remain a needed virtue in the future.

7

Christian Gratitude to Nurture a Thankful Life

THE VIRTUE OF GRATITUDE moves us to acknowledge some good action or kindness that we have received, leading us to express this in some way of thankfulness. Examples abound. A child receives a long-desired toy on Christmas morning and (perhaps due to a parent) will ultimately write a thank-you note to the giver. A business executive who has received a promotion due in part to a positive recommendation from someone chooses an appropriate way to acknowledge the courtesy. Or perhaps a woman who unexpectedly receives flowers from her significant other and whispers a simple yet heartfelt "thank you, my love." Gratitude is perhaps more popularly considered as a social grace that, when absent or forgotten, renders human society a little less civilized.

Christian gratitude moves Christian disciples to render thanks to God as the source for, in a word, everything. Gratitude moves us to express this in prayers of praise or thanksgiving in some way, whether in words of prayer or, more deeply, through lives that reflect our faithful following of Jesus.

I. GRATITUDE THROUGH THE HISTORY OF CHRISTIAN SPIRITUALITY

In Scriptures

The biblical texts illustrate that thanksgiving was a central part of the spiritual experience for both Jews and Christians, sharing the desire to render thanks to God for the many blessings they had received. While the Christian understanding viewed their salvation as coming from the life of Jesus, both spiritual bodies exhorted their members to be grateful for God's goodness to them.

The Old Testament

Gratitude for God's gifts, above all for the Exodus from Egypt, and the ways to express thanksgiving for them, are at the heart of the Hebrew experience of God. Thankfulness is frequently conveyed among the writings of the Old Testament in verses that praise, give thanks, or otherwise glorify God.

The Hebrews' delivery from bondage in Egypt marked the beginning of a new phase in their relationship with God who, for them, had honored the covenant made with Abraham. The people were instructed to remember annually God's great action in the Passover feast, a time of praise and wonderment in which they would recall Moses' song after their rescue from the pursuing soldiers. Henceforth they gave thanks to God through their recalling and making ritually present the memory of God's mighty deed of deliverance from the Egyptians:

> I will sing to the LORD, for he has triumphed gloriously; horse and rider he has thrown into the sea.
> The LORD is my strength and my might, and he has been my salvation; this is my God, and I praise him;
> my father's God, and I will exalt him . . .
> You brought them in and planted them on the mountain of your own possession,
> the place, O LORD, where you made your abode, the sanctuary, O LORD, that your hands have established.
> The LORD will reign forever and ever.[1]

---

1. Exod 15:1–2; 17–18.

God had proven to be faithful and trustworthy through leading the people of Israel to freedom.

The Jewish offering from their firstfruits from their first harvest in the promised land captured two interesting facets of their intention. First, the offering was made in thanksgiving to God for God's blessing of the people by way of land and produce; the second was the people's recognition that their blessings came from God, a portion of which they returned to God in the form of an oblation:

> A wandering Aramean was my ancestor; he went down into Egypt and lived there as an alien, few in number, and there he became a great nation, mighty and populous. When the Egyptians treated us harshly and afflicted us . . . we cried to the LORD, the God of our ancestors; the LORD heard our voice and saw our affliction, our toil, and our oppression. The LORD brought us out of Egypt with a mighty hand and an outstretched arm . . . So now I bring the first of the fruit of the ground that you, O LORD, have given me.[2]

So many of the Old Testament psalms serve to bolster the people's faithfulness through recalling God's continual providential care for them during times of both happiness and hardship. For example, the first psalm asserts that the person who chooses to walk in the way of the Jewish law and follows not the path of the wicked shall be happy, noting in the final verse that "the LORD watches over the way of the righteous, but the way of the wicked will perish." The Hebrews not only proclaimed gratitude for God's faithfulness for themselves alone but also shared their gratitude with the surrounding nations, as in the short Psalm 117: "Praise the LORD, all you nations; extol him, all you peoples! For great is his steadfast love toward us, and the faithfulness of the LORD endures forever."

This firm belief in God's ultimate justice and deliverance motivated the Hebrew people to praise God at all times, whether in joyful moments or in those that brought suffering, exile, and persecution. Not that they gave some perverse offering of thanks for the chance to suffer. Rather, their praise expressed confidence in God's ultimate and proven victory over any evil, and that the God who had accompanied them through so much past suffering and despair continued with them even in their present tribulation. Job, for example, contrary to the advice given by his wife (Job 2:9), blessed God during the time of his misfortune in saying "the LORD gave, and the LORD has taken away; blessed be the name of the LORD" (1:21).

---

2. Deut 26:5–10.

As another example is the pious Tobit who had performed a charitable deed of burying a dead stranger; later, while resting, he became blinded. Although he at first he prayed to God for death, Tobit remained steadfast in his trust of God's ways for him and his family, realizing in the end that the divine hand had been at work through their difficulties of life.

The Jewish scriptural religious tradition collectively expresses the community gratitude and thankfulness for all blessings received; for their land and the produce that it afforded to them, for the blessings of age that came with children and their children's children, for God having led them into God's light and away from the darkness of the surrounding pagan peoples. Most especially, though, we find the people celebrating God's ongoing covenant with them in prayer and ritual thanks. God had proven faithful time and time again; in response, the people were commanded to express their gratefulness through obedience in fulfilling the terms of the Covenant and by never forgetting God's goodness and blessings. In the Jewish thanksgiving or *todah* offering, unleavened bread was offered to God and consumed by the people, while a portion was set aside and given to God as a sustenance offering to the temple priests.

The New Testament

The earliest Christian regard for gratitude varied considerably from the surrounding cultures. Gifts given and received in the Greco-Roman world formed an understood relationship between giver and recipient, with an expectation of remuneration according to the significance of the gift and according to particular circumstances. This attitude had considerable influence on people in society, civil government, family life, and their relationship with pagan deities. The effects and varying outlooks toward the practice are too complex to explore at length in this short chapter but must be acknowledged when considering the uniqueness of Christian gratitude.[3]

The gospel message tended to subvert this fundamental attitude of society, perhaps adding to the popular perception that Christianity was deleterious to it. Rather than owing reciprocity to another person, Christians gave primacy of thanksgiving to God, the source and sustainer of all creation and blessings. This foundational Christian ideal became co-opted as the interpersonal gift-reciprocity relationship would reemerge in different

---

3. For a more detailed treatment, see Leithart, *Gratitude*, chapters 1–2.

Christian Gratitude to Nurture a Thankful Life

forms over subsequent Christian history through evolving philosophical, societal, and political thought.

The New Testament contains many manifestations of praise and thankful prayer to God. In the Lord's Prayer (Matt 6:9–13), Jesus taught his disciples that praise of God should be a foundational part of their daily prayer. They should begin with simple praise ("Our Father in heaven, hallowed be your name"), along with submitting to the mysterious Reign of God that was unfolding in their midst ("your kingdom come, your will be done on earth as it is in heaven"). Praise and thanksgiving to his heavenly Father was a prime motivator for Jesus in completely turning his life over to the Father's loving plan, exclaiming "I thank you, Father, Lord of heaven and earth, because you have hidden these things from the wise and the intelligent and have revealed them to infants; yes, Father, for such was your gracious will."[4]

Luke's Gospel contains a notable emphasis on the place and importance of gratitude and thanksgiving in one's relationship with God. The angel's annunciation to Mary of her impending divine motherhood leads her to visit her cousin Elizabeth, also with child, where Mary expresses in her canticle the joy of all Israel in God's constant faithfulness (1:46–55). Zacharias praises God for God's faithfulness when his tongue is loosened (1:63–79). The family visit to the temple following Jesus' birth and his presentation to both Simeon and Anna likewise invokes God's faithful blessing of the Jewish people (2:28–38).

In the Lukan account of Jesus' ministry, Jesus encounters ten lepers who approach him for healing (17:11–19). Jesus grants their desire with a mere thought in their direction and a simple sending-forth to the priest who would pronounce them cleansed; one of them, a religiously outcast Samaritan, realizes he has been healed and returns alone to Jesus to praise and thank him for his new life. Jesus asks why only a foreigner has returned to give thanks rather than the others (presumably children of Israel); in so doing, Luke seems to highlight the rightfulness of Christian praise and gratitude to God for divine blessings.[5]

In several letters, the apostle Paul emphases the importance of praise and thanksgiving for those who embrace the Christian way. Gratitude should fill the Christian's life: "Rejoice always, pray without ceasing, give

---

4. Luke 10:21; see Wright, *Theology of Christian Prayer*, 19.

5. The Lukan Acts of the Apostles 2:46–47 also notes that the early Jerusalem Christians offered daily praise to God.

thanks in all circumstances; for this is the will of God in Christ Jesus for you" (1 Thess 5:16–18). The Pauline Epistles show frequent expressions of thankfulness to God for the spiritual blessings he had observed in his various communities. Echoing a common convention of Hebrew and Greek writing, Paul's first letter to the Corinthians typifies this while centering his praise on the generosity of the risen Christ:

> I give thanks to my God always for you because of the grace of God that has been given you in Christ Jesus, for in every way you have been enriched in him, in speech and knowledge of every kind . . . as you wait for the revealing of our Lord Jesus Christ. He will also strengthen you to the end, so that you may be blameless on the day of our Lord Jesus Christ. God is faithful; by him you were called into the fellowship of his Son, Jesus Christ our Lord.[6]

Paul's writing also reflects his praise of God even in moments of adversity. His letter to the Galatians, primarily a rebuke and a reaffirmation of their newfound faith in Christ, nevertheless bears his recognition of the goodness they all have received by way of their salvation: "Grace to you and peace from God our Father and the Lord Jesus Christ, who gave himself for our sins to set us free from the present evil age."[7] Despite the disputed Pauline authorship of Ephesians, the first chapter contains notes of thanksgiving and praise for God's marvels that the community had experienced through the apostolic ministry and in its spiritual blessings.

We note, in conclusion, that the Scriptures offer many examples of both communal and individual praise and thanksgiving to God. These are in recognition of divine faithfulness or other benefits that God had bestowed on the people from the days of their earliest spiritual ancestors, primarily giving thanks for their salvation that God had rendered throughout their long history. Even in times of hardship and suffering, devout individuals express thankfulness for God's continual accompaniment, responding with renewed obedience to the law of the Covenant. The earliest Jewish Christian communities followed this tradition while recognizing Jesus as the fulfillment of God's promise of salvation.

---

6. 1 Cor 1:4–9.
7. Gal 1:3–5.

Gratitude in the Patristic Era

The Church Fathers

True to the form of the lived spirituality found in early Christianity, we find that patristic exhortations to thankfulness appear in a number of sources from the later first through the sixth centuries, for a variety of reasons.

A frequent reason for gratitude among the church fathers during the first three centuries is appreciation for the gift of the Christian faith in their world surrounded by pagan and other non-Christian influences. Clement of Rome exhorted his listeners of troubled Corinth to respect the faith of one another by which they had been saved from darkness and death:

> Let us therefore reflect, brethren, of what clay we were made, what and who we were when we entered the world, out of what grave and darkness our Maker and Creator has brought us into the world, where He had prepared His benefits before our birth. Since, then, we owe all these blessings to Him, we are obliged to thank Him in every way. To Him be the glory forever and evermore. Amen.[8]

The second-century *Didache* gives a precious glimpse into Christian life and prayer among the early Christians of Syria. By this time, Christian exhortation to personal thanksgiving in prayer had become to some extent ritualized in the still-developing Christian bread-breaking ritual, the Greek word for "thanksgiving," *eucaristia*, eventually adopted by the Latin West. In their celebrations, the *Didache* instructed Christians first to collectively offer thanks to God for the basic gifts of wine and bread presented as a thanksgiving offering and channel of unity with other Christian communities:

> First, in connection with the cup, "We give Thee thanks, Our Father, for the holy vine of David Thy son, which Thou hast made known to us through Jesus Thy Son; to Thee be glory forever. And in connection with the breaking of bread, "We give thee thanks, Our Father, for the life and knowledge which Thou hast revealed to us through Jesus Thy Son; to Thee be glory forever." As this broken bread was scattered upon the mountain tops and after being harvested was made one, so let thy Church be gathered together

---

8. 1 Clem. 38.

from the ends of the earth into thy kingdom, for Thine is the glory and the power through Jesus Christ forever.[9]

Following their partaking of the blessed offerings, the document also instructs the community to be thankful for the gift of their faith and for God's benevolence toward them:

> Give thanks in the following way: "We thank thee, Holy Father, for Thy holy name, which Thou has caused to dwell in our hearts and for the knowledge and faith and immortality, which Thou hast made known to us through Jesus thy Son; to Thee be glory forever. Thou, Lord almighty, has created all things for Thy name's sake and hast given food and drink and eternal life through Thy son. For all things we render Thee thanks, because Thou art mighty; to Thee be glory forever.[10]

In another part of the Christian world, Irenaeus of Lyons also recognized that Christians should offer lives of gratitude to God for the faith they have received, made possible by God's long-suffering patience for their return:

> This, therefore, was the [object of the] long-suffering of God, that man, passing through all things, and acquiring the knowledge of moral discipline, then attaining to the resurrection from the dead, and learning by experience what is the source of his deliverance, may always live in a state of gratitude to the Lord, having obtained from Him the gift of incorruptibility, that he might love him the more.[11]

But God, Irenaeus asserted, does not expect mere cereal or meat offerings; transformed lives and hearts in accordance with God's law offer the thanksgiving sacrifice that truly pleases God:

> And again, when He points out that it was not for this that He led them out of Egypt, that they might offer sacrifice to Him, but that, forgetting the idolatry of the Egyptians, they should be able to hear the voice of the Lord, which was to them salvation and glory, He declares by this same Jeremiah: "Thus says the Lord; Collect together your burnt-offerings with your sacrifices, and eat flesh. For I spoke not unto your fathers nor commanded them in the day that I brought them out of Egypt, concerning burnt-offerings or sacrifices: but this word I commanded them, saying, Hear My

---

9. Did. 9.
10. Did. 10.
11. Irenaeus, *Haer.* 3.20.2.

voice, and I will be your God, and you shall be My people; and walk in all My ways whatsoever I have commanded you, that it may be well with you.[12]

Not surprisingly, the early church fathers also instructed on prayer in many places; how to pray, why to pray, where, etc. Throughout, we find an attitude of thanksgiving to God as a normal component of one's expressions of prayer and praise to God. This expression, as Origen wrote to the Christian antagonist Celsus, was chiefly through living in a way conformable to God's commands; doing so underscores our rightful nature with respect to God our creator and source of all that we receive, who blesses us exceedingly:

> But we, while recognising the duty of thankfulness, maintain that we show no ingratitude by refusing to give thanks to beings who do us no good, but who rather set themselves against us when we neither sacrifice to them nor worship them. We are much more concerned lest we should be ungrateful to God, who has loaded us with His benefits, whose workmanship we are, who cares for us in whatever condition we may be, and who has given us hopes of things beyond this present life. And we have a symbol of gratitude to God in the bread which we call the Eucharist.[13]

The Christian eucharistic offering, at once simple and sublime, outwardly expresses our thankfulness to God and prompts us to express it more intimately through our transformed lives.

From the fourth century, Christian liturgy and prayer found their roots in the Eastern churches that continued the traditional appreciation of thanksgiving as an essential ingredient from its earliest foundation. The so-called "Cappadocian Fathers" contributed much to early theological and liturgical development. Basil of Caesarea composed at least one sermon that treated of the importance of thanksgiving in prayer, along with considerable practical insight. To Christians who were weak or lacking belief, or other naysayers who ask how could a disciple give thanks to God in moments of suffering, loss, etc., Basil recalled to them that the apostle Paul exhorted Christians to rejoice always. Basil noted that our joy comes from our faith; while our losses produce sadness, these are ordinary consequences of human life. Such moments should not quench our joy and thankfulness, following the Old Testament example of Job when he declared, in the midst of

---

12. Irenaeus, *Haer.* 4.17.3.
13. Origen, *Cels.* 8.57.

his misery of loss and suffering, that "the LORD gave, and the LORD has taken away; blessed be the name of the LORD" (Job 1:21). Basil repeated the patristic viewpoint to his audience that nothing happens in our life without God's awareness of it. These trials will come along in their designated time; we should be prepared for them and not let them overwhelm the basic joy that comes from our underlying faith and experience of God through Jesus.[14]

Basil's younger brother, the contemplative Gregory of Nyssa (ca. 335–ca. 395), stated more bluntly why we should give glory and thanksgiving to God: We owe everything to God; our very life came into being through the divine goodness by whom we are held in present existence, and who provides our hope for future bliss through our remembering God's goodness during the course of our life. Indeed, we have only our prayer and attitude of thanksgiving to offer to God, as insufficient as they may be, in which we simply proclaim our recognition of the great store of unmerited divine blessings that we have received.[15]

In the West, the late fourth-century *Confessions* of Augustine of Hippo notes his gratitude at having been delivered from the folly of his younger days, realizing that without God's grace he would have been lost in his own desires and pursuits:

> Bear with me, I beg, and permit me to follow round in present memory the past courses of my error and to offer Thee a sacrifice of rejoicing. For, what am I for myself, without Thee, but a guide unto destruction? Or what am I, when all is well with me, but one suckling on Thy milk and enjoying Thee, the food incorruptible? And what is man, any man, since he is but a man?[16]

Augustine recognized that his way of remaining in an attitude of thankfulness was to remember that we are creatures and God is our creator, always deserving of our love and subjection as imperfect beings, to whom we should direct our entire self, to the One Who offers true happiness; otherwise, we shall ultimately reap unhappiness with lesser goods:

> The farther, then, the mind departs from God, not in space, but in affection and lust after things below Him, the more it is filled with folly and wretchedness. So by love it returns to God—a love which places it not along with God, but under Him. And the more ardor and eagerness there is in this, the happier and more elevated will

---

14. Basil, "Homily of Thanksgiving," 22–29.
15. First sermon on the Lord's Prayer. Gregory of Nyssa, "Lord's Prayer," 21–34.
16. Augustine, *Conf.* 4.1.

the mind be, and with God as sole governor it will be in perfect liberty. Hence it must know that it is a creature. It must believe what is the truth—that its Creator remains ever possessed of the inviolable and immutable nature of truth and wisdom, and must confess, even in view of the errors from which it desires deliverance, that it is liable to folly and falsehood.[17]

We nurture this love for the Triune God through our praise of God as our greatest good:

> We ought then to love God, the Trinity in unity, Father, Son, and Holy Spirit; for this must be said to be God Himself, for it is said of God, truly and in the most exalted sense, "Of whom are all things, by whom are all things, in whom are all things." Those are Paul's words. And what does he add? "To Him be glory." All this is exactly true. He does not say, To them; for God is one. And what is meant by, To Him be glory, but to Him be chief and perfect and widespread praise? For as the praise improves and extends, so the love and affection increases in fervor. And when this is the case, mankind cannot but advance with sure and firm step to a life of perfection and bliss.[18]

Our examination of the early patristic-era contributions has uncovered a number of insights concerning the value of gratitude in early Christianity. One is that Christian disciples had reason to be grateful to God for the gift of their faith, helping to guide them through the many obstacles and the spiritual darkness of their age. A second value is for expressing gratitude for God's divine patience as a way to stretch their faith and grow in obedience. Third, as Jesus held an attitude of thanksgiving to the Father, so his disciples should follow his example. Finally, we find that collective Christian expressions of thanksgiving soon became ritualized in the Eucharistic liturgy and as a fundamental element of Christian prayer.

From the fourth century, Christian writers emphasized a few additional points. One was that we rightfully owe our gratitude and respect to God as the source of all blessings and, indeed, for life itself in one's Christian duty to God. In faith, we should accept both blessings and difficulties in a spirit of gratitude; nothing happens without God's being aware of it, and these moments of hardship can help in our ongoing formation into

---

17. Augustine, *Mor. eccl.* 21.
18. Augustine, *Mor. eccl.* 24.

ever-more-faithful and mature disciples. Finally, our thankful praise of God can help to deepen our love for God.

Gratitude in the Medieval Era

Christian Monasticism

The regimen of early Christian monks substantially institutionalized the Christian call to thankfulness. The first monks learned the psalms for daily recitation in their quest for a unified life that included Paul's exhortation to pray always and give thanks (1 Thess 5:16–18). The Eastern monastic practices found their way into the West beginning in the fourth century. Cassian's *Conferences* (ninth book) taught that true thanksgiving to God in prayer was a rather high achievement, requiring a quelling of interior passions to reach "purity of heart" along with detachment from any desire of personal gain. Western communities of monks had begun to form by the year 400, and the daily Benedictine communal liturgical prayer services, known as the *opus Dei* or "work of the Lord," included psalms of praise.

Western monastic life, with its emphasis on communal liturgical prayer and learning, became the practical locus for Western spiritual writing and practice. Expressing gratitude and thanksgiving, while a universal Christian value for all Western medieval disciples, became largely absorbed into monastic piety and asceticism through the twelfth century. Most of the surrounding laity (the great majority of the Christian church!) would have been all but excluded due to their non-participative presence in eucharistic celebrations, liturgical celebrations in unfamiliar Latin, and the low degree of education and catechesis. Greater lay participation in Christian spiritual life would begin to reemerge by the thirteenth century, thanks largely to Church renewal efforts among religious orders such as the Franciscans, Dominicans, and many lay associations.

The Later Medieval Period

The twelfth through fourteenth centuries witnessed an outburst of Christian mystical thought and experiences that displayed a pervasive, active, and lively sense of gratitude among many mystics of those centuries. Expressions of Christian spirituality had also begun to move beyond the

Christian Gratitude to Nurture a Thankful Life

boundaries of monastic life; one source for active gratitude is evident among the writings of Francis of Assisi.

Francis's rule of 1221, written for his spiritual family, instructed the Franciscan brothers to give thanks to God in praise for every good accomplishment; praise was also a fitting response to whatever evil the friars encountered during their day, as we find in the seventeenth section:

> We must refer every good to the most high supreme God, acknowledging that all good belongs to him; and we must thank him for it all, because all good comes from him. May the most supreme and high and only true God receive and have and be paid all honour and reverence, all praise and blessing, all thanks and all glory, for to him belongs all good and *no one is good but only God* (Luke 18:19). And when we see or hear people speaking or doing evil or blaspheming God, we must say and do good, praising God, who is blessed for ever.[19]

Indeed, Francis exhorted his brothers to offer praise and thanksgiving to God whenever the situation warranted it (section 21), not only in prayer but also through seeking transformed lives:

> Whenever they see fit my friars may exhort the people to praise God with words like these: Fear him and honour him, praise him and bless him, thank and adore him, the Lord almighty, in Trinity and unity, Father, Son, and Holy Spirit, Creator of all. *Repent, for the kingdom of heaven is at hand* (Mt. 3:2); remember we must soon die . . . It is well for those who die repentant; they shall have a place in the kingdom of heaven. Woe to those who die unrepentant; they shall be children of the devil whose work they do, and they shall go into everlasting fire. Be on your guard and keep clear of all evil, standing firm to the last.[20]

The rule also includes a final proclamation of praise and thanksgiving to God for all that God accomplishes, for the Franciscan life as a means to salvation for the individual friar, and an exhortation to God the Father that Jesus and all the saints continue to offer eternal and fitting praise to their heavenly Father.[21]

Among his other writings, Francis's composition *The Canticle of Creation* underscores what he perceived as a continual praise to God that is

---

19. Franciscan rule of 1221, chap. 17. Habig, *St. Francis of Assisi*, 45.
20. Franciscan rule of 1221, chap. 21. Habig, *St. Francis of Assisi*, 46–47.
21. Franciscan rule of 1221, chap. 23.

offered by the innumerable elements of the created world. In sum, Francis of Assisi offered a way of life in which praise and thanksgiving to God were foundational.

Gratitude among the Fourteenth Century Mystics

In England, the fourteenth-century anchoress (solitary) Julian of Norwich (1342–ca. 1416) recorded in the *Showings of Divine Love* her views and experiences of prayer and her deep love-filled relationship with God. Along with petitionary prayer, thanksgiving was an important element. In petitionary prayer ("beseeching"), we express our dependence on God for what we need and request, an attitude that pleases God and so invites further divine blessings; thankful prayer allows us to express our gratitude to God for what we have received. Julian's work relates that there are three especially important items for which we should give thanks to God: "The first is our noble making, the second our precious and loveable redemption, the third everything which he has made inferior to us to serve us and which he protects for love of us."[22]

A second locale of spiritual fruitfulness was in the *Imitation of Christ*. In several places, the book instructs readers to express their gratitude to God as the source of all gifts. Readers should be grateful for spiritual graces moving them to humility. They should also accept even moments of suffering or hardship; since God is the source of whatever comes to them, each moment holds some measure of spiritual profit that can help deliver them to their final salvation (2.10). They should be thankful for every benefit they have since everything they possess comes from God's blessing, most especially for their clarity in following God's plan for oneself (3.22). The final section focuses on the enormity of the Eucharistic gift and calls the recipient to deep thankfulness for Christ's body and blood contained in the species of bread and wine.

The third area of development occurred in the Tuscan hills of Italy, where the mystical experiences of Catherine of Siena (1347–80) are recorded among her collected letters and in her *Dialogue*. Catherine underscored the importance of having gratitude in one's daily life in at least one letter, seeing that cultivating gratitude would lead to growth in other virtues, writing that:

---

22. Julian of Norwich, *Showings of Divine Love* 42 (long text). See Colledge and Walsh, *Julian of Norwich*, 252.

> I, Catherine, servant and slave of the servants of Jesus Christ, write to you ... desiring to see you grateful and appreciative of the benefits you have received from your Creator, so that the spring of piety may be fed within you. This gratitude will make you eager to practise virtue, for while ingratitude makes a soul lazy and negligent, this sweet gratitude makes it so hungry for time that every hour, every moment, sees it at work. All true virtue comes from this gratitude, for what else but gratitude gives us charity, or makes us humble and patient? Seeing the immense debt it owes to God, the [grateful] soul does its best to live virtuously, knowing that God asks only this.[23]

Elsewhere, Catherine wrote that gratitude to God could be best expressed through one's assiduous obedience to God's laws.[24]

Gratitude in the Modern Era

The five hundred years of the Modern Era also supported appreciation for the quality of Christian gratitude. The later period also produced a gradual movement away from its traditional Christian roots toward more socially-conditioned applications of gratitude in later disciplines such as political philosophy and psychology.

Early Reformation Influences

Martin Luther placed a strong accent on the place of thankfulness in the life of a Christian. He intended his "small catechism" to be a pastoral aid to bishops in response to what he saw as widespread ignorance of basic tenets of Christian life; in this document we find several entries that illustrate Luther's emphasis on regular thanksgiving. Christians should not take the name of the Lord in vain; rather, they should fear and love God, calling upon God through prayer, praise and thanksgiving.[25] God as Father Almighty is the source of one's earthly and spiritual blessings; for this we owe to God our thanks, praise, service, and obedience,[26] and from whom

---

23. May 8, 1379 letter to Bartalo Usimbardi and Francesco di Pippino, of Florence. Catherine of Siena, "Letter to Bartalo Usimbardi," 230.
24. Catherine of Siena, *Dial.* 163.
25. Luther, "Small Catechism," 121–22.
26. Luther, "Small Catechism," 123.

we should likewise receive our daily bread with thanksgiving.[27] Christians should also render thanks to God following their morning rising and prior to evening sleep, before and after meals.

The foundation for John Calvin's experience of God included a deep appreciation for God's majesty and absolute greatness, the source of all life and blessing, who is all-deserving of Christian gratitude and thankfulness. Calvin compared the intensity of God's vast love for humanity in terms of the extreme loving suffering of a woman in labor.[28] The divine greatness, thus, naturally elicits from us a movement of praise and thankfulness for God's greatness, something we should proclaim at all times, in response to whatever we may receive from the greatness of God, its source. Thankfulness, for Calvin, was foundational to growth in piety and obedience to God:

> We must be persuaded not only that as [God] once formed the world, so he sustains it by his boundless power, governs it by his wisdom, preserves it by his goodness, in particular, rules the human race with justice and judgment, bears with them in mercy, shields them by his protection; but also that not a particle of light, or wisdom, or justice, or power, or rectitude, or genuine truth, will anywhere be found, which does not flow from him, and of which he is not the cause; in this way we must learn to expect and ask all things from him, and thankfully ascribe to him whatever we receive... For, until men feel that they owe everything to God, that they are cherished by his paternal care, and that he is the author of all their blessings, so that nought is to be looked for away from him, they will never submit to him in voluntary obedience; nay, unless they place their entire happiness in him, they will never yield up their whole selves to him in truth and sincerity.[29]

The sixteenth-century Spanish Catholic reform period also emphasized cultivating the virtue of gratitude. Francisco de Osuna (1492 or 1497—ca. 1540), a Franciscan, asserted early in his *Third Spiritual Alphabet* that those intent on maturing in the ways of recollection prayer and the deeper reaches of recollection-based mysticism should foster an attitude of thankfulness from the very beginning. His work offers a beautiful picture of how the rest of creation expresses a natural gratitude to God, something easily lost among human beings:

---

27. Luther, "Small Catechism," 124.
28. Calvin, *Commentary on Isaiah*, 302–3.
29. Calvin, *Institutes* 1.2.1.

Christian Gratitude to Nurture a Thankful Life

> We see that when earth is regaled by heaven's waters and sunlight, it sends forth grass and flowers in grateful payment for the gift. Very tenderly the gardener cares for his trees so that, having grown quite tall, they bend down their fruit for him to pick, almost as if to say: "Take this fruit in return for your kind care." And when the little birds sing and chirp in greeting to the sun, who is to say that they do not sing thanks to the sun for coming with light and happiness to free them from the cold and peril of the night?[30]

Osuna recognized that the virtue has two dimensions: one is that which God supernaturally nourishes in our soul, and the other form that we are able to cultivate through individual ascetical effort (his primary focus). He repeated that Christian disciples have reason to give thanks to God for *everything* that comes into our lives. We should give thanks not only for our pleasant blessings; rather, we should also acknowledge hardships, difficulties, and sorrows since God, although not *willing* our sufferings, nevertheless *permits* them to come our way. In such moments, we are to unite our sufferings with the sufferings of Christ on the cross and be thankful for even these experiences that God may use to help form our maturing discipleship and ultimately realize our eternal salvation.[31]

The Third Spiritual Alphabet influenced many notable figures in the tradition of Christian spirituality; among them was Teresa of Avila. Teresa's autobiography expresses many thankful praises to God for not having abandoned her in her perceived moments of immature unfaithfulness. Teresa repeats in several points of her gratitude to God for the many manifestations of God's goodness found in God's mercy, God's patience, and God's desire that all be saved and find the fullness of life in their union.

> I often marveled to think of the great goodness of God, and my soul delighted in seeing His amazing magnificence and mercy. May He be blessed by all, for I have seen clearly that He does not fail to repay, even in this life, every good desire. As miserable and imperfect as my deeds were, this Lord of mine improved and perfected them and gave them value, and the evils and sins He then hid . . . He gilds my faults; the Lord makes a virtue shine that He himself places in me—almost forcing me to have it.[32]

---

30. de Osuna, *Third Spiritual Alphabet* 2.1.
31. de Osuna, *Third Spiritual Alphabet* 2.4.
32. Teresa, *Life* 4.10.

Teresa's gratitude to God is also apparent among her other major works, a natural expression of her oft-stated close friendship with God in Jesus.

The spirituality of Francis de Sales expresses some of his attractive personal joy and optimism, in contrast to other French spiritual movements of his day, and continues to influence the spiritual lives of Christian disciples in our own time. Francis wrote in his *Introduction to the Devout Life* that Christian disciples should reflect on God's goodness to them in order to elicit a deeper gratitude toward God. Early in the book, de Sales calls the prayerful person to reflect on all the gifts from God that he or she has received physically (a physical body, health); next, to consider the blessings of one's education and mental abilities; then to give thanks to God for the many spiritual gifts and remedies that are available (sacraments, etc.) that assist them toward their final salvation. After reflecting on God's goodness to disciples, de Sales instructs them to reflect on their own degree of ingratitude. Finally, disciples should make a conscious resolution of thankfulness to God.[33]

Some three centuries later, Thérèse of Lisieux (1873–97) believed that she should treat every day as a chance to give God profound thanksgiving for her blessings. Remembering to do this seemed to draw additional ones, concluded Thérèse, echoing the experiences of past Christian mystics in words recounted by her sister Celine, also a Carmelite nun:

> It is the spirit of gratitude which draws down upon us the overflow of God's grace . . . for no sooner have we thanked Him for one blessing than He hastens to send us ten additional favors in return. Then, when we show our gratitude for these new gifts, He multiplies His benedictions to such a degree that there seems to be a constant stream of divine grace ever coming our way . . . This has been my own personal experience; try it out for yourself and see. For all that Our Lord is constantly giving me, my gratitude is boundless, and I try to prove it to Him in a thousand different ways.[34]

Other Emanations of Christian Gratitude

We have identified many of the significant spiritual reasons and attitudes for cultivating the Christian virtue of gratitude from the viewpoint of the longer Christian tradition. Other developments also have had their effect,

33. de Sales, *Introduction* 1.11.
34. Martin, *Memoir of My Sister Saint Thérèse*, 97.

for better or worse. These have emerged in both reformed Christianity and among more marginally Christian philosophical developments that were fruits of the eighteenth-century Enlightenment period, influencing the fields of religious, political, and economic theory.

As theologian Peter J. Leithart notes, Reformation and post-Reformation Christianity initially sought to regard gratitude, gift, and reciprocity to the gift from a limited sense of the gospel tradition as handed down by Jesus and Paul, continuing a misunderstanding that was already present in some pre-Reformation Christian thought. This helped to produce an imbalanced view of gift and reciprocity in some social and political philosophies over the next centuries, due in part to the undesirable tendency of gift-giving to carry with it some feeling of personal indebtedness (i.e., lack of freedom) on the part of the receiver. Other Enlightenment thinking led to a view of social thought that marginalized the place of God in one's understanding of gifts as divine blessings. By the nineteenth century, in short, the distorted understanding of Christian gratitude was compromised for the sakes of individualism, personal and political autonomy, and economic systems.[35] These results have all taken their toll on the popular contemporary appreciation of gratitude.

On the cusp of the contemporary era, we find that the lived experience of Christian spirituality provides several traditional reasons for cultivating the virtue of gratitude. One is that thankfulness expressing gratitude belongs as a foundation stone of Christian prayer. Christians should frequently express thanksgiving to God for gifts received, including the less-recognized "gifts" of misfortune and suffering, since God can use these, too, for our spiritual benefit. An additional thought is that growth in gratitude will increase our sense of humility before God, thereby inciting our greater personal fidelity and obedience to God's laws and transformed lives.

II. TOWARDS A CONTEMPORARY APPRECIATION FOR CHRISTIAN GRATITUDE

Much has been written of gratitude in the present day from the perspective of both nonreligious scientific thought as well as from spiritual perspectives. From a psychological viewpoint, Emma Greene notes in *The Atlantic* that there are plenty of beneficial psychological reasons for cultivating

---

35. See Leithart, *Gratitude*, 8–15.

gratitude, considered more as a human emotion rather than the classically-understood sense of virtue:

> The social science on gratitude is pretty resolute: Feeling thankful is good for you. "There's something called a grateful personality that some psychologists have studied," said Jo-Ann Tsang, a psychologist at Baylor University. "They find that if you're greater in the grateful personality, you tend to have increased life satisfaction, happiness, optimism, hope, positive emotion, and . . . less anxiety and depression." . . . Other studies suggest that diaries, daily reminders, and intentional reflection on what you're thankful for can boost happiness, positive emotions, and a sense of meaning in life, Tsang said. Physical benefits may include fewer symptoms of illness and better sleep. These activities "can even help people with moderate body-image issues, and also people with moderate anxiety issues," she added.[36]

Indeed, gratitude is among the most-studied human qualities, recognized as an important ingredient for personal happiness and mature self-adjustment, a focus of "positive psychology."[37] Psychotherapist Amy Morin has noted at least seven positive benefits for developing the "attitude of gratitude" in terms of overall happiness, relationships, physical and psychological health, improved sleep, reduced aggressiveness, self-esteem, and mental strength or resilience.[38]

Gratitude among other World Religions

Expressing thankfulness to the divine through prayer is certainly found among the major world religions. One quickly realizes that many justifications for gratitude-based prayer strike a resonant chord with traditional Christian and Judeo-Christian reasons. In Hinduism, for instance, adopting an attitude of thanksgiving can bring the praying person closer to the deities:

> The purpose of any prayer in Hinduism is to express your gratitude to the gods, make mental offerings to them, and keep your mind filled with divine thoughts. When you fill your mind with the thoughts of gods in prayers, you manifest them in your

---

36. Green, "Gratitude Without God," ll. 5–14.

37. See, for instance, Leithart, *Gratitude*, 220; or some of the essays contained in the work by Emmons and McCullough, *Psychology of Gratitude*.

38. Morin, "7 Scientifically Proven Benefits Of Gratitude."

consciousness, and their qualities and virtues begin to strengthen in you. Prayers awaken your divinity and improve your karma. They are your wings to the worlds of gods.[39]

Gratitude in Hindu prayer can also include gratitude for difficult challenges that have come into one's life, helping to mold the person into a better one:

> Sometimes just being grateful for experiencing failure, makes you see it as a gift. It is a stepping stone from which you can revisit your goals and expectations. It is an excellent opportunity to realise that when one door closes, many windows open. When you look at the year gone by, celebrate both the ups and downs. These experiences have contributed to your growth this year.[40]

Buddhism offers another example. Having gratitude in one's "mindfulness" helps practitioners to situate themselves as part of their wider world; this, in turn, aids in developing personal generosity and forgiveness of others:

> Practicing mindfulness of gratitude consistently leads to a direct experience of being connected to life and the realization that there is a larger context in which your personal story is unfolding. Being relieved of the endless wants and worries of your life's drama, even temporarily, is liberating. Cultivating thankfulness for being part of life blossoms into a feeling of being blessed, not in the sense of winning the lottery, but in a more refined appreciation for the interdependent nature of life. It also elicits feelings of generosity, which create further joy. Gratitude can soften a heart that has become too guarded, and it builds the capacity for forgiveness, which creates the clarity of mind that is ideal for spiritual development.[41]

The Islamic appreciation for gratitude has much in common with traditional Jewish and Judeo-Christian thought. Gratitude to God is considered a foundational duty owed to Allah; a maturing appreciation for gratitude will gradually move from gratitude in one's heart, to one's lips in vocal proclamation, and finally one's gratitude should produce righteous deeds toward one's neighbor.[42] We find something of this intention on the lips of the prophet

---

39. V., "Few Thoughts About Prayers in Hinduism," para. 14.
40. Shyam, "Attitude of Gratitude," para. 8.
41. Moffitt, "Selfless Gratitude," para. 3.
42. Karim, "Concept of Thankfulness in Islam," ll. 41–43.

Abraham, recounting to nonbelievers his hope in Allah who enables Abraham to live. No other god is like that of Abraham, he declares:

> Not so the Lord and Cherisher of the Worlds;
> Who created me, and it is He who guides me;
> Who gives me food and drink, and when I am ill, it is He who cures me;
> Who will cause me to die, and then to live (again);
> And who, I hope, will forgive me my faults on the Day of Judgement.[43]

Gratitude in the Writing of Contemporary Christian Spirituality Writers

Among contemporary Christian writers, one finds a range of thought on the value of cultivating gratitude. Thomas Merton, in his few references to gratitude, recognized that gratitude was foundational in growing to know God, that "our knowledge of God is perfected by gratitude: we are thankful and rejoice in the experience of the truth that He is love."[44] We owe everything to our Creator, Merton asserts:

> To be grateful is to recognize the Love of God in everything He has given us—and He has given us everything. Every breath we draw is a gift of His love, every moment of existence is a grace, for it brings with it immense graces from Him. Gratitude therefore takes nothing for granted, is never unresponsive, is constantly awakening to new wonder and to praise of the goodness of God. For the grateful man knows that God is good, not by hearsay but by experience. And that is what makes all the difference.[45]

While gratitude itself is a specific concept, several authors have addressed the related idea of gratefulness. David Steindl-Rast (1926–) has produced several works addressing gratefulness and its relationship to gratitude. Gratitude, he observes, will elicit from us one of two basic responses depending on whether it is from a personal encounter or beyond. One set of responses may be labeled as thankfulness, typically directed to the benefactor of a gift that is deliberately and specifically given to someone. Gratefulness is what Steindl-Rast assigns to the second class, the more diffusive and spontaneous appreciative feelings that arise from the

---

43. *Qur-An* Suret 26, A.77–82.
44. Merton, *Thoughts in Solitude*, 41.
45. Merton, *Thoughts in Solitude*, 43.

joy of observing a beautiful sunset, a mountaintop view, or other moments that can result in what are called mystical or "peak experiences," and less-significant moments.[46] Gratefulness produces a spontaneous movement of thanks for experiencing the unexpected joy and appreciation for certain moments in life as unmerited gifts that, unless the recipient is more attuned to them, often pass unacknowledged.[47]

Two additional authors—Mary Jo Leddy *(Radical Gratitude,* 2002) and Susan Muto *(Gratefulness,* 2018)—explore the value of gratefulness as fitting for contemporary Christian discipleship. Fostering a grateful attitude to God for all of one's gifts and experiences, including the more difficult ones, strengthens a Christian disciple to live more at peace and better able to persevere in our western society that is assailed by consumerism and personal consumption.

Gratitude in Relationship to God, One Another, and in Creation

We can appreciate that the virtue of gratitude enjoys considerable attention in a variety of fields, whether religious or not. Christians, of course, look to the example of Jesus and how later Christian generations have tried to incorporate it over two millennia. At root, we find several traditional reasons for cultivating gratitude as created human beings. In our concentric view of discipleship, we find:

With God

We have at least three elements to note that argue for developing the virtue of gratitude in one's life. One is that gratitude inspires a person to an attitude of thankfulness toward God, a foundational attitude in a disciple's life of prayer. Gratitude reinforces our sense of humility in recognizing that each of us is, in the end, utterly dependent on God for all that we have; even our next breath or the gift of tomorrow morning are experiences that we take for granted but are never guaranteed.

Our Creator is the source of all we have; above all, we have reason to be grateful for our Christian faith and guidance as we journey through life in our contemporary day that can seem to be a whirlwind of evolution

---

46. Steindl-Rast, "Gratitude as Thankfulness and as Gratefulness," 282–89.
47. Steindl-Rast, *Gratefulness, the Heart of Prayer,* 9–25.

and change. Scientific and industrial technology inexorably draw us with promises of a simplified life, but at what cost? The breakneck pace of advancement and change tends to outrun the development of fitting ethical principles, sometimes leaving us to feel that society has deviated considerably from any Christian-based ethic concerning the value of individual human life, family life, the dignity of human work, etc. Christians have reason to be thankful for the life example of Jesus, whose way of love offers us a pathway to follow in an uncertain world.

We can also be grateful that God accompanies us at all times during our life, in moments of both joy and sorrow; whether in the soaring exhilaration of completing a long-awaited goal, in the crushing agony of losing a child or spouse, or somewhere in-between. In whatever our experience, we can give thanks to God as one who walks with us in every moment; in some of life's more bitter experiences, it may require much time to do so. As we gradually emerge from the pain of loss, we can often find that our personal perception of God in our world has somehow broadened as our basic faith in God has been tested and tempered.

With Others

Our basic gratitude toward God for blessings will naturally grow to include gratitude for other people. Human relationships are central to what it means to be a person, and normally our range of friendships will necessarily narrow itself as we consider our actual breadth of acquaintances from the more casual variety, then to our closer friends, finally passing to those few more intimate relationships and perhaps a lifelong spouse. Whether we share with others the events of our daily life, our dreams and ambitions, or our spiritual yearnings, we have good reason to be grateful to God for the persons to whom we can reveal our deeper selves and who allow us to experience theirs.

No doubt there are some personal acquaintances whom we might not welcome as "blessings." But even those who irritate us can be the source of other blessings in our lives, perhaps giving us the opportunities to grow in such qualities as patience, compassion, or understanding. A wise monk said somewhere that a truly good monastic community life will include not only a congenial monk with whom he got along well, but also the one or two disagreeable individuals that challenge him to grow in Christian charity.

Finally, developing an attitude of gratitude in life can bear fruit in our Christian vocation to extend the reign of God in the world. Growing in gratitude tends to make us more attractive to others, resulting in our being perhaps more approachable (even sometimes becoming more tolerable to *them*!). As Augustine of Hippo observed, the world can become a better place through our growth in gratitude.[48]

With Creation

From the most obvious to the most sublime, everything we receive, everything around us, every belief that we can sense or conceptualize or claim as a result of faith: everything is God's gift. Gratefulness for the small joys of creation around us can lead us to appreciate that all of creation is full of both large and small marvels that, in their beauty or delicateness or complexity, are capable of reflecting some attribute of their divine source. Bees and butterflies, seashores and sunsets, sparrows and spider webs, forests and flowery fields . . . Just as a human gift can tell us something about the giver, so every gift to us from our surrounding world is capable of expressing something of the divine Giver, whether in random beauty or in showing us something of the divine genius that unfolds around us today and has marvelously done so since the beginning.

As with other virtues that we have considered in this book, exercising gratitude in our lives helps us to grow in respecting that the gifts surrounding us are also meant for the good of all. *Laudato Si'* captures something of this in its longer final thanksgiving prayers:

> Father, we praise you with all your creatures.
> They came forth from your all-powerful hand;
> they are yours, filled with your presence and your tender love.
> Praise be to you!
> ~~~~~
> Triune Lord, wondrous community of infinite love,
> teach us to contemplate you
> in the beauty of the universe,
> for all things speak of you.
> Awaken our praise and thankfulness
> for every being that you have made.
> Give us the grace to feel profoundly joined

---

48. Augustine, *Mor. eccl.* 24.

to everything that is.[49]

Everything we have, everything that we are, come freely from our divine Source who merits our thankfulness and praise. Lives guided by Christian gratitude can help to counter the numbing effects of personal autonomy and individualism in our society that can regard personal blessings and gains of life and creation as matters of personal and national entitlement, rather than as fragile yet marvelous gifts from the One who breathes being and life into us all. Gratitude sincerely expressed through our thankfulness for God's gifts offers a counterwitness and a thwart to the ingratitude often at work in contemporary human lives that dismisses the giftedness of God, the joy and even passion of relationships, and the reality that each one of us is among the host of God's gifts filling our created world.

---

49. Francis, *Laudato Si'*, no. 246.

Bibliography

Adnés. "Humilité." In *Dictionnaire de Spiritualité: Ascétique et Mystique, Doctrine et Histoire*, edited by Marcel Viller et al., 6:1136-87. Paris: Beauchesne, 1968.
à Kempis, Thomas. *The Imitation of Christ*. Translated by Ronald Knox and Michael Oakley. New York: Sheed & Ward, 1959.
Ambrose of Milan. "On the Duties of the Clergy." In *NPNF2* 10:1-89.
Arundel, Morgan. "Patience—A Spiritual Virtue." http://www.yogaesoteric.net/content.aspx?lang=EN&item=6595.
Athanasius of Alexandria. "The Life of Anthony." In *Early Christian Biographies*, edited by Roy J. Deferrari, 133-216. Fathers of the Church 15. Washington, DC: Fathers of the Church, 1952.
Augustine of Hippo. "Confessions." In *Saint Augustine: Confessions*, translated by Vernon J. Bourque, 45-207. Fathers of the Church 21. New York: Fathers of the Church, 1953.
———. "Exposition on Psalm 147." In *Expositions of the Psalms: 121-50*, edited by Boniface Ramsey, 441-75. The Works of Saint Augustine: a Translation for the 21st Century 3.20. Hyde Park: New City, 2008.
———. "Letter 23" (*Maxim.*). In *Letters 1-99*, edited by John E. Rotelle, 63-68. The Works of Saint Augustine: A Translation for the 21st Century 2.1. Hyde Park: New City, 2001.
———. "On the Good of Marriage" (*Bon. conj.*). In *Marriage and Virginity: The Excellence of Marriage, Holy Virginity, the Excellence of Widowhood, Adulterous Marriages, Continence*, edited by John E. Rotelle, 33-61. The Works of Saint Augustine: A Translation for the 21st Century 1.9. Hyde Park: New City, 1999.
———. "On the Morals of the Catholic Church." In *NPNF1* 4:41-63.
Aumann, Jordan. *Spiritual Theology*. London: Sheed & Ward, 1980.
Baasten, Matthew. "Humility and Modern Ethics." *Reformed Review* 38.3 (1985) 232-37.
Bacchi, Lee F. "A Ministry Characterized by and Exercised in Humility: the Theology of Ordained Ministry in the Letters of Augustine of Hippo." In *Augustine: Presbyter Factus Sum*, edited by Joseph T. Lienhard et al., 405-15. Collectanea Augustiniana. New York: Lang, 1993.
Baker, Derek, ed. *Medieval Women*. Oxford: Blackwood, 1978.
Balthasar, Hans Urs Von. "The Poverty of Christ." *Communio* 13.3 (1986) 196-98.
Basil of Caesarea. "Homily of Thanksgiving." Translated by Hieromonk Patapios. *Orthodox Tradition* 17.4 (2000) 22-29.

Bibliography

———. *On Social Justice: St Basil the Great*. Translated by C. Paul Schroeder. Popular Patristics Series 38. Crestwood, NY: St. Vladimir's Seminary Press, 2009.

Bernard of Clairvaux. "Sermon 36." In *Bernard of Clairvaux: on the Song of Songs II*, translated by Kilian Walsh, 173–80. Cistercian Fathers Series 7. Kalamazoo: Cistercian, 1976.

———. "Sermon 42." In *Bernard of Clairvaux: on the Song of Songs II*, translated by Kilian Walsh, 210–19. Cistercian Fathers Series 7. Kalamazoo: Cistercian, 1976.

Bilezikian, Gilbert. "Discipline." In *Baker* 2:631–33.

Brundage, James A. *Law, Sex, and Society in Medieval Europe*. Chicago: University of Chicago Press, 1987.

Calvin, John. *Commentary on the Book of the Prophet Isaiah*. Translated by William Pringle. Calvin's Commentaries 8. Grand Rapids: Baker, 2003.

———. *Institutes of the Christian Religion by John Calvin*. Translated by Henry Beveridge. Grand Rapids: Eerdman, 1993.

Casey, Michael. "The Virtue of Patience in Western Monastic Tradition." *Cistercian Studies* 21.1 (1986) 3–23.

Cassian, John. *John Cassian: The Conferences*. Translated by Boniface Ramsey. Ancient Christian Writers 57. New York: Paulist, 1997.

———. *John Cassian: The Institutes*. Translated by Boniface Ramsey. Ancient Christian Writers 58. New York: Newman, 2000.

Catechism of the Catholic Church: Revised in Accordance with the Official Latin Text, Promulgated by Pope John Paul II. 2nd ed. Washington, DC: United States Catholic Conference, 1997.

Catherine of Siena. *The Dialogue*. Translated by Suzanne Nofke. Classics of Western Spirituality. New York: Paulist, 1980.

———. Letter to Bartalo Usimbardi and Francesco di Pippino of Florence, dated May 8, 1379. In *I, Catherine: Selected Writings of St. Catherine of Siena*, edited and translated by Kenelm Foster and Mary John Ronayne, 230–32. London: Collins, 1980.

Chrysostom, John. "Homily 30" (on Acts 13). In *NPNF1* 11:188–94.

———. "Homily Concerning Lowliness of Mind" (*Prof. evang.*). In *NPNF1* 9:147–55.

———. "On the Priesthood." In *NPNF1* 9:33–83.

———. "On Virginity." In *John Chrysostom: On Virginity: Against Remarriage*, translated by Sally Reiger Shore, 1–128. Studies in Women and Religion 9. New York: Edwin Mellen, 1983.

———. "Sermon on Marriage." In *St. John Chrysostom: On Marriage and Family Life*. Translated by Catherine P. Roth and David Anderson, 81–88. Crestwood, NY: St. Vladimir's Seminary Press, 1986.

Ciraulo, Jonathan Martin. "Thomas Merton's Creative (dis)Obedience." *Cistercian Studies Quarterly* 46.2 (2011) 89–219.

Clement of Alexandria. *Stromateis*. In *Clement of Alexandria: Stromateis Books One to Three*. Translated by John Ferguson. Fathers of the Church 85. Washington: Catholic University of America Press, 1991.

Clement of Rome. *1 Clement*. In *The Epistles of St. Clement of Rome and St. Ignatius of Antioch*. Translated by James A. Kleist, 9–49. Ancient Christian Writers 1. Westminster, MD: Newman, 1946.

Cyprian of Carthage. "On the Advantage of Patience." In *ANF* 5:484–91.

———. "On the Discipline and Advantage of Chastity" (*Util. disc.*). In *ANF* 5:587–92.

———. "On the Dress of Virgins" (*Hab. virg.*). In *ANF* 5:430–36.

Bibliography

———. "On the Lapsed." In *Saint Cyprian: Treatises*, edited and translated by Roy J. Deferrari et al., 57–88. Fathers of the Church 36. New York: Fathers of the Church, 1958.

de Osuna, Francisco. *Third Spiritual Alphabet*. Edited and translated by Mary Giles. New York: Paulist, 1981.

de Sales, Francis. *Introduction to the Devout Life*. Edited and translated by John K. Ryan. New York: Image, 1989.

"Didache." In *The Apostolic Fathers*, edited and translated by Francis X. Glimm et al., 171–84. Fathers of the Church 1. New York: Cima, 1947.

Egan, Harvey. *Christian Mysticism: The Future of a Tradition*. New York: Pueblo, 1984.

Emmons, Robert, and Michael McCullough, eds. *The Psychology of Gratitude*. New York: Oxford University Press, 2004.

Faricy, Robert. "Teilhard de Chardin's Spirituality of the Cross." *Horizons* 3.1 (1976) 1–15.

Francis. *Laudato Si'*. http://w2.vatican.va/content/francesco/en/encyclicals/documents/papa-francesco_20150524_enciclica-laudato-si.html .

Genovesi, Vincent. "Sexuality." In *The New Dictionary of Theology*, edited by Joseph A. Komonchak et al., 947–54. Collegeville: Liturgical, 1993.

George, Robert. "Gnostic Liberalism." *First Things* (December 2016) 33–38.

Goodrich, Richard. "John Cassian on Monastic Poverty: The Lesson of Ananias and Sapphira." *Downside Review* 124 (2006) 297–308.

Green, Emma. "Gratitude Without God: If Giving Thanks Isn't Inherently Religious, Where Does It Come From?" *The Atlantic*, November 26, 2014. https://www.theatlantic.com/health/archive/2014/11/the-phenomenology-of-gratitude/383174/.

Gregory of Nyssa. "The Lord's Prayer: Sermon 1." In *St. Gregory of Nyssa: The Lord's Prayer; The Beatitudes*, translated by Hilda C. Graef, 21–34. Ancient Christian Writers 18. Westminster: Newman, 1954.

Gregory the Great. *Gregory the Great: Pastoral Care*. Translated by Henry Davis. Ancient Christian Writers 11. New York: Newman, 1950.

Grundmann, Walter. "ταπεινός." In *TDNT* 8:1–26.

Habig, Marion, ed. *St. Francis of Assisi: Writings and Early Biographies*. Chicago: Franciscan Herald, 1973.

Hinson-Hasty, Elizabeth. "Revisiting Feminist Discussions of Sin and Genuine Humility." *Journal of Feminist Studies in Religion* 28.1 (2012) 108–14.

Hitchcock, James. "The Emergence of the Modern Family." In *Christian Marriage: A Historical Study*, edited by Glenn W. Olsen, 302–31. New York: Crossroad, 2001.

Holzherr, Georg. *The Rule of Benedict: An Invitation to the Christian Life*. Translated by Mark Thamert. Cistercian Studies Series 256. Collegeville: Liturgical, 2016.

Ignatius of Antioch. *The Epistles of St. Clement of Rome and St. Ignatius of Antioch*. Translated by James A. Kleist. Ancient Christian Writers 1. Westminster, MD: Newman, 1946.

Ignatius of Loyola. *Letters of St. Ignatius of Loyola*. Translated and edited by William Young. Chicago: Loyola University Press, 1959.

———. "Spiritual Exercises." In *Ignatius of Loyola: Spiritual Exercises and Selected Works*, edited by George Ganss, 121–24. New York: Paulist, 1991.

Irenaeus of Lyons. "Against the Heresies" (*Haer.*). In *ANF* 1:315–567.

Jedin, Hubert, and John Dolan. *History of the Church*. 10 vols. New York: Crossroad, 1980–81.

Jerome. "Against Vigilantius." In *NPNF2* 6:417–23.

Bibliography

John Paul II, Pope. *Pastores Dabo Vobis.* http://www.vatican.va/content/john-paul-ii/en/apost_exhortations/documents/hf_jp-ii_exh_25031992_pastores-dabo-vobis.html.

———. *Vita Consecrata.* http://www.vatican.va/content/john-paul-ii/en/apost_exhortations/documents/hf_jp-ii_exh_25031996_vita-consecrata.html.

Johnson, Rick. "The Old Testament Demand for Faith and Obedience." *Southwestern Journal of Theology* 32.3 (1990) 27–35.

Julian of Norwich. *Julian of Norwich: Showings.* Translated by Edmund Colledge and James Walsh. New York: Paulist, 1978.

Justin Martyr. "1 Apology." In *ANF* 1:163–87.

Kadloubovsky, E., and G. E. H. Palmer. *Early Fathers from the Philokalia.* London: Faber & Faber, 1954.

Karim, Fatima. "The Concept of Thankfulness in Islam." *Medium* (blog), May 22, 2018. https://medium.com/@Marytn/the-concept-of-thankfulness-in-islam-b16e9e40332a.

Konkola, Kari. "Have We Lost Humility?" *Humanitas* 18.1–2 (2005) 182–207.

Lactantius. "Divine Institutes." In *ANF* 7:9–223.

Leithart, Peter J. *Gratitude: An Intellectual History.* Waco, TX: Baylor University Press, 2014.

Liebert, Elizabeth. *The Way of Discernment: Spiritual Practices for Decision-Making.* Louisville: Westminster John Knox, 2008.

Lindberg, Carter. "Luther on Poverty." *Lutheran Quarterly* 15.1 (2001) 85–101.

Luther, Martin. "Small Catechism." In *A Reformation Reader: Primary Texts and Instructions,* edited by Denis R. Janz, 118–29. 2nd ed. Minneapolis: Fortress, 2008.

Martin, Céline. *A Memoir of My Sister Saint Thérèse.* New York: Kenedy, 1959.

Merton, Thomas. *Thoughts in Solitude.* New York: Doubleday, 1958.

Miller, Frederick L. "Saint Philip Neri and the Priesthood." *Homiletic & Pastoral Review* 109.4 (2009) 8–17.

Moffitt, Phillip. "Selfless Gratitude." *DharmaWisdom* (blog), 2011. http://dharmawisdom.org/teachings/articles/selfless-gratitude.

Morin, Amy. "7 Scientifically Proven Benefits Of Gratitude That Will Motivate You to Give Thanks Year-Round." *Forbes,* November 23, 2014. https://www.forbes.com/sites/amymorin/2014/11/23/7-scientifically-proven-benefits-of-gratitude-that-will-motivate-you-to-give-thanks-year-round/#2571ef29183c.

Mulhern, Philip. *Dedicated Poverty: Its History and Theology.* Staten Island, NY: Alba, 1973.

"Nine Beliefs of Hinduism." *Hinduism Today,* February 22, 2008. https://www.hinduismtoday.com/modules/wfchannel/index.php?wfc_cid=19.

Olsen, Glenn W. *Christian Marriage: A Historical Study.* New York: Crossroad, 2001.

———. "Marriage in Barbarian Kingdom and Christian Court: Fifth through Eleventh Centuries." In *Christian Marriage: A Historical Study,* edited by Glenn W. Olsen, 146–212. New York: Crossroad, 2001.

Origen of Alexandria. "Against Celsus." In *ANF* 4:395–669.

Palladius of Aspuna. *The Lausiac History.* Translated by John Wortley. Cistercian Studies Series 252. Collegeville: Liturgical, 2015.

Paul VI, Pope. *Gaudium et Spes.* http://www.vatican.va/archive/hist_councils/ii_vatican_council/documents/vat-ii_const_19651207_gaudium-et-spes_en.html.

———. *Lumen Gentium.* http://www.vatican.va/archive/hist_councils/ii_vatican_council/documents/vat-ii_const_19641121_lumen-gentium_en.html.

Bibliography

———. *Perfectae Caritatis*. http://www.vatican.va/archive/hist_councils/ii_vatican_council/documents/vat-ii_decree_19651028_perfectae-caritatis_en.html.

———. *Populorum Progressio*. http://w2.vatican.va/content/paul-vi/en/encyclicals/documents/hf_p-vi_enc_26031967_populorum.html.

———. *Presbyterorum Ordinis*. http://www.vatican.va/archive/hist_councils/ii_vatican_council/documents/vat-ii_decree_19651207_presbyterorum-ordinis_en.html

Pierre, Teresa Olsen. "Marriage, the Body, and Sacrament in the Age of St. Victor." In *Christian Marriage: A Historical Study*, edited by Glenn W. Olsen, 213–68. New York: Crossroad, 2001.

Pius IV. *Benedictus Deus*. https://en.wikisource.org/wiki/Canons_and_Decrees_of_the_Council_of_Trent/Second_Part/Bull_of_our_most_Holy_Lord_Pius_Fourth.

Porter, Jean. "Natural Equality: Freedom, Authority and Obedience in Two Medieval Thinkers." *Annual of the Society of Christian Ethics* 21 (2001) 275–99.

Pseudo-Clement. "Letter to Virgins." In *ANF* 8:55–60.

Quinn, Arthur G. "Continence and Celibacy in the Early Christian Community." *Homiletic and Pastoral Review* 104.8 (2004) 42–50.

Rabgye, Karma Yeshe. "The Virtue of Patience." *Buddhism Blog*, July 11, 2014. http://buddhismguide.org/the-virtue-of-patience/.

Reardon, Patrick Henry. "The Man Alive: Irenaeus Did Not Teach Self-Fulfillment." *Touchstone*, September-October 2012. https://www.touchstonemag.com/archives/article.php?id=25-05-003-e.

Reynolds, E. E. *The Trial of Saint Thomas More*. New York: J. Kenedy & Sons, 1964.

Rolheiser, Ronald. *The Holy Longing: The Search for a Christian Spirituality*. New York: Doubleday, 1999.

Russell, Norman, trans. *The Lives of the Desert Fathers*. Cistercian Studies Series 34. Kalamazoo: Cistercian, 1980.

Sands, Paul. "The Deadly Sin of Pride." *Journal of Family and Community Ministries* 23 (2010) 40–49.

Shyam, Anuradha. "An Attitude of Gratitude." *The Hindu*, January 5, 2014. https://www.thehindu.com/features/education/an-attitude-of-gratitude/article5538332.ece.

Siepierski, Paolo. "Poverty and Spirituality: Saint Basil and Liberation Theology." *Greek Orthodox Theological Review* 33.3 (1988) 321–26.

Smither, Edward L. *Missionary Monks*. Eugene, OR: Cascade, 2016.

Soble, Alan. "Philosophy of Sexuality." https://www.iep.utm.edu/sexualit/.

Spanneut, Michel. "Le Stoïcisme dans l'Histoire de la Patience Chrétienne." *Mélanges de Science Religieuse* 39.3 (1982) 101–30.

Steenberg, M. C. "Impatience and Humanity's Sinful State in Tertullian of Carthage." *Vigilae Christianae* 62 (2008) 107–32.

Steindl-Rast, David. *Gratefulness, the Heart of Prayer*. Ramsey, NJ: Paulist, 1984.

———. "Gratitude as Thankfulness and as Gratefulness." In *The Psychology of Gratitude*, edited by Robert Emmons and Michael McCullough, 282–89. New York: Oxford University Press, 2004.

Stenzel, Meinrad. "Poverty." In *EBT* 2:671–73.

Stöger, Alois. "Humility." In *EBT* 2:385–90.

Taylor, Jeremy. *The Rule and Exercise of Holy Living*. Philadelphia: Bradley, 1860.

Teilhard de Chardin, Pierre. *The Divine Milieu: An Essay on the Interior Life*. New York: Harper & Row, 1975.

Bibliography

Teresa of Avila. *The Collected Works of St. Teresa of Avila.* Vol. 1, *The Book of Her Life, Spiritual Testimonies, Soliloquies.* Translated by Kieren Kavanaugh and Otilio Rodriguez. Washington, DC: ICS, 1976.

Tertullian. "Against Marcion" (*Marc.*). In *ANF* 3:269–475.

———. "To His Wife" (*Ux.*). In *Tertullian: Treatises on Marriage and Remarriage*, translated and annotated by William P. Le Saint, 10–36. Ancient Christian Writers 13. Westminster, MD: Newman, 1951.

———. "Of Patience." In *ANF* 3:707–17.

———. "On Flight from Persecution" (*Fug.*). In *ANF* 4:116–25.

Thompson, Edward Healy. *The Life of Jean-Jacques Olier: Founder of the Seminary of St. Sulpice.* London: Burns & Oates, 1885. https://archive.org/stream/lifeofolieroothomuoft?ref=ol#page/n6/mode/2up.

Thompson, William M. *Bérulle and the French School: Selected Writings.* Classics of Western Spirituality. New York: Paulist, 1989.

Ullathorne, William Bernard. *Christian Patience, the Strength and Discipline of the Soul.* London: Burns and Oates, 1886. https://archive.org/details/ChristianPatience/page/n5.

V., Jayaram. "A Few Thoughts About Prayers in Hinduism." https://www.hinduwebsite.com/ask/how-to-pray.asp.

Van Bavel, T. J. "The Evangelical Inspiration of the Rule of St. Augustine." *Downside Review* 93 (1975) 83–99.

Van Engen, John. *Devotio Moderna: Basic Writings.* Mahwah, NJ: Paulist, 1988.

Weaver, Rebecca H. "Wealth and Poverty in the Early Church." *Interpretation* 41.4 (1987) 368–81.

Wilcock, Michael J. "Poor, The." In *Baker* 4:1732–33.

Wright, John H. *A Theology of Christian Prayer.* Pueblo, CO: Glazier, 1987.

Name Index

Abel, 6
Abraham (Abram), 5, 28, 47, 156
Adam, 8, 47, 49, 59
Alexander III, Pope, 124
Aquinas, Thomas. *See* Thomas Aquinas.
Ambrose of Milan, 122
Amos, 25
Anna, 26, 139
Anthony of Egypt, 32, 100
Athanasius, 100
Augustine of Canterbury, 123
Augustine of Hippo, 31, 80–82, 84, 86, 102, 144–45, 159

Basil of Caesarea, 80, 100–101, 110, 143–44
Becket, Thomas, 123–24
Benedict of Nursia, 12, 33, 54, 80
Bernard of Clairvaux, 12, 34, 83–84
Bérulle, Pierre de, 37, 106
Boleyn, Anne, Queen, 126
Bonaventure, 35–36
Bonhoeffer, Dietrich, 63, 130
Brigid of Ireland, 104

Calvin, John, 14, 150
Campion, Edmund, 127
Cassian, John, 11, 32–33, 53, 103, 146
Catherine of Aragon, Queen, 126
Catherine of Siena, 105, 148–49
Celsus, 29
Chrysostom, John, 30, 80–82, 99
Clare of Assisi, 105
Clark, Maura, 63

Clement of Alexandria, 76–77, 98
Clement of Rome, 6, 28, 50–51, 75, 141
Columban (Columbanus), 104, 123
Constantine, 53
Cyprian of Carthage, 8–9, 16, 78–80, 98–99

David, King, 28, 70, 116
Day, Dorothy, 63, 109–10, 130
de Osuna, Francisco, 150–51
de Sales, Francis, xii, 15, 58–59, 152
Dominic of Guzman, 105
Doms, Herbert, 87
Donovan, Jean, 63

Eleazar, 117
Elizabeth (cousin of Mary), 139
Elizabeth I, Queen, 126–27
Eve, 8, 47, 59
Ezekiel, 116

Felicitas (Felicity), 120–21
Ford, Ita, 63
Francis, Pope, 45, 67, 93, 159–60
Francis of Assisi, 105, 147–48,
Frederick I, Emperor, 123

Gandhi, Mahatma, 130
Garrigou-Legrange, Reginald, xii
Green, Emma, 153–54
Gregory of Nyssa, 144
Gregory the Great, Pope, 12, 83, 123
Groot, Geert, 13
Gutierrez, Gustavo, 111

Name Index

Henry II, King, 124
Henry VIII, King, 126–27
Hildebrand, Dietrich von, 87
Hugh of St. Victor, 84
Hus, John, 105

Ignatius of Antioch, 29, 75, 119–20
Ignatius of Loyola, 37, 57, 65
Irenaeus of Lyons, 52, 142–43
Isaac, 47

Jerome, 80, 102
Job, 3, 28, 137, 143
John Paul II, Pope, 21, 88–89, 108–9
Judith, 25
Julian of Norwich, 148
Justin Martyr, 75–76

Kant, Immanuel, 86
Kazel, Dorothy, 63
King, Rev. Martin Luther, Jr., 63, 130

Lactantius, 10, 11
Lazarus, 26, 96, 99
Leddy, Mary Jo, 157
Liebert, Elizabeth, 65
Leithart, Peter J., 153
Louis II, King, 124
Luther, Martin, 56, 86, 106, 149–50

MacIntyre, Alistair, xii
Martin, Céline, 152
Mary (mother of Jesus), 26, 117–18, 139
Mary I, Queen, 126–27
Maurin, Peter, 109
McCain, John, 130
Melanie the Elder, 100
Merton, Thomas, 63, 156
More, Thomas, Sir, 126–27
Morin, Amy, 154
Moses, 2, 5, 47, 136
Muto, Susan, 157

Nathan, 70
Neri, Philip, 106
Nixon, Richard M., President, 62
Noah, 5

Olier, Jean-Jacques, xii, 15–16, 38, 59, 106–7
Origen, 29, 75, 143

Pachomias, 80
Paul (of Tarsus), 4, 6, 26–27, 41, 49, 72–75, 97, 101, 118, 122, 139–40, 146
Paul VI, Pope, 20, 88–89, 108, 110–11
Perpetua, 120–21
Peter (Simon), 6, 50, 118
Pius IV, Pope, 57
Pius XI, Pope, 87
Pius XII, Pope, 87
Plato, 29, 86
Polycarp of Smyrna, 10, 119
Pseudo-Clement, 76

Reynolds, E. E., 127
Rodriguez, Alphonsus, xii
Rolheiser, Ronald, 68
Romero, Oscar, 63
Russell, Bertrand, 86

Saul, 6
Simeon, 139
Solomon, 116
Stang, Dorothy, 63, 133
Steindl-Rast, David, 156–57

Tanquerey, Adolph, xii
Taylor, Jeremy, 38–39
Teilhard de Chardin, Pierre, 18–19
Teresa of Avila, 14, 129, 151–52
Teresa of Calcutta, 129
Tertullian, 7–9, 16, 77–78, 121
Thérèse of Lisieux, 66, 152
Thomas Aquinas, xii, 55, 84–85, 125–26
Thompson, Edward Healey, 60
Tobit, 138

Ullathorne, W. B., 16

Victor IV, Pope, 124

www.ingramcontent.com/pod-product-compliance
Lightning Source LLC
Chambersburg PA
CBHW050809160426
43192CB00010B/1701